The Tender Touch

reaching out, building relationships

Rexella Van Impe

Thomas Nelson Publishers

Nashville

Second Printing

Copyright © 1980 by Jack Van Impe Crusades

Published in Nashville, Tennessee, by Thomas Nelson, Inc., Publishers and distributed in Canada by Lawson Falle, Ltd., Cam-
bridge, Ontario.

Scripture quotations are from *The King James Version*.

Library of Congress Cataloging in Publication Data

Van Impe, Rexella.
   The tender touch.

   1. Van Impe, Rexella.   2.   Van Impe, Jack.
3. Evangelists—United States—Biography.   I.   Title.
BV3785.V34A36   269'.2'0922 [B]   80-24593
ISBN   0-8407-5745-X

To my loving husband, whose
Spirit-filled life has made
it easy for me to express
"the tender touch."

CONTENTS

FOREWORD

For twenty-nine years, I have experienced the blessed privilege of personally serving my Lord and Savior, walking daily by His side and by the side of one of His choice servants—my husband, Dr. Jack Van Impe, "The Walking Bible." In some respects, the years have been long and difficult. In other ways, they have passed quickly. They have been precious years—years of victory and personal fulfillment. I wouldn't trade them for anything; if I could, I would relive them a thousand times.

During our local church campaigns, the great city-wide crusades and, more recently, our radio and television ministries, we have been honored to enter the hearts and lives of millions. Hundreds have often remained behind following the close of our services in order to become better acquainted with our ministry. Multiplied thousands have written personal letters which we were thrilled to receive and rejoiced in answering. You see, we have wanted to get to know you better, too.

Personally, I have wanted to share intimately God's love, power, and provision with every woman I have met. Yet the time has always been so short.

This book is my most personal letter ever—written *especially for you*. Through it I hope to let you know me better, and perhaps you will come to know yourself better as well. I pray that the thoughts I share will bring us ever so much closer together, and help you to know all that you can be through Christ.

Lovingly,

Rexella

1

This Is What
It Is Like to Die

It was a gloriously happy day! Jack and I strolled the sidewalks of Brussels, browsing through the quaint shops of this medieval city. Many years had passed since my first visit to Belgium as a young bride. We had celebrated our first anniversary aboard ship, returning to America after spending three months with my mother- and father-in-law in their missionary outreach. I loved Belgium, the home of my husband's ancestors. There had been other trips to this fascinating country, but this vacation was special—a gift from World Tours for our twenty-seventh wedding anniversary.

Time had magnified the countryside's charm and brushed the landscape with luster. Fit for a painter's canvas were the rolling mountains carpeted with lush foliage, and the serene valleys carved by rivers and canals. The portrait was completed by windmills turning and farmers in wooden shoes laboring in the fields.

What a contrast to Brussels, a bustling, cosmopolitan city that is headquarters of the Commission of European Communities (the Common Market). Favorite tourist sites are the King's Palace and the Tomb of the Unknown Soldier; the Atomium constructed for the 1958 World's Fair exhibition; the museums housing collections of gifted Flemish artists; and the impressive cathedrals, centers of worship for the population, which is 98 percent Roman Catholic.

There is always a festive mood at the magnificent square known as Grand Place; it preserves the Old World charm in its ancient buildings with elaborate gold leaf design. The market is a cascade of color, as carts of fresh flowers and vegetables are brought in daily from the countryside.

Relaxing over lunch at a little outdoor cafe, we caught a glimpse of the world hurrying down the cobblestone streets. But my husband and I were in a world of our own as we reminisced—twenty-seven years of walking together with the Lord.

"Honey, we've always had such good times together," Jack said.

Oh, yes! They were good years. We had teased and laughed, talked and listened, quibbled and forgiven, loved and grown—truly one in the Lord. A fairy-tale marriage? Maybe, but it had not been without its share of pain and disappointment. Many times we had waded through deep waters, clinging to each other and to God's promises that we would not be swept away.

We could rejoice this August afternoon in 1979. In two days we would fly home to Michigan and plunge into our new weekly television ministry, which was being launched in faith to reach America for Christ. But first we would enjoy an anniversary celebration with Jack's relatives in Belgium. A cousin was preparing a feast, and it was time to be on our way.

Jack was driving his uncle's small car. As we approached an intersection, something came speeding up behind us at fifty miles an hour.

"A bus! Jack! There's a bus!"

He swerved the car to the left, but it was too late. I placed my arm on the door to brace myself and the bus struck us from the rear. It ripped away the right side of the car and flung me into the busy street. My head hit violently on the pavement.

So this is what it is like to die!

I feel no fear or pain, only the sweetest peace.

I'm dying . . . stepping over to be with Him!

Something warm is on my face . . . Jack's tears . . . he's praying.

"Oh, God, please help us. Somehow spare her life!"

I'm slipping away from him. I must tell him how much I love him.

"Honey, I believe I am dying and I don't want to leave you!"

A hand is grasping my wrist . . . a stranger is beside me. Someone is putting a blanket over me.

"Don't move her."

Is he just a man, or a ministering angel sent by God to comfort us?

Such comfort! My mind is clearing. I sense a great assurance that I will live! Jack must know!

"Honey, I'm going to be all right!"

2

Living by the Rules But Lost

I was born in Clarkton, Missouri, cotton country south of the Ozarks and near the Arkansas line. Ours was a very secure and peaceful home that reflected the touch of gentle, godly parents.

My mother, Esther, was a petite, soft-spoken woman with boundless energy. The house was always in order, the laundry always done. She never missed a service at church, and she always had energy enough to love us all. One of my earliest memories is of her singing . . . I must have been still in her arms.

Perhaps that is why I grew to love music, too. By age six I was singing in church, introducing the songs myself. Mother never allowed me to look at words as I sang; the songs must be memorized. When I started piano lessons, she required me to practice every day before I went out to play—a half hour at first and an hour when I was older. This early discipline was invaluable preparation for my future.

Balancing Mother's quiet disposition was Dad's fun-loving nature. Rex Shelton was a big man (at six-foot-one, he was the shortest son in his family), but he was very tender. He wasn't afraid to say he loved us and to show it. Nothing was asking too much; he would have gone through fire for his children. And such patience! Without a word of complaint he would take me to church five times if I needed to rehearse a song, and he never minded if I were the last to leave.

He has always been a great father. He was always there whenever I needed him. I was named after him and loved him deeply. He was the head of our home and a tower of strength. During the Great Depression, Dad left his business in Clarkton to move the family to Pontiac, Michigan, where he worked in the insurance business. Later he took a job as a truck inspector at General Motors.

I grew up between two brothers: Bob, who is three and a half years older than I, and Don, who is four years younger. We were very close. Bob knew the Lord from childhood and never rebelled. Don and I so admired and respected him that we would have done anything he asked. Every Saturday the three of us went to the movies. I "mothered" Don, choosing balcony seats so he wouldn't be frightened by scary scenes. Then, as a teen-ager, Bob became convicted about going to the movies and stopped.

"Shall I stop?" I asked him.

"Let your conscience guide you," he said.

"But Bob," I said as I realized it for the first time, "you are my conscience." He was a figurehead representing my faith and a very important aspect of my life.

Obedience was instilled in us as children. Although my parents were strict, they disciplined with enormous love. Talking to me was sufficient discipline. For them to say they were disappointed in me hurt tremendously. I deeply respected them and rarely wanted to disobey.

How grateful I am that my parents built self-confidence into my life. Not one day went by without my mother and father telling me they loved me. Whenever I prepared for a date Dad would tell me how nice I looked. (This is very important to a young girl; Daddy's approval is the first approval of the opposite sex.) Their generous love made my childhood immensely secure. Both were born-again believers and faithful members of a Baptist church. Above all, they set an example of love and loyalty to Christ and His Word.

A Christian home is a great heritage for a child, but it can harbor a hidden danger—knowing all about Jesus without knowing Him personally as Savior.

When I was twelve, I joined the First Baptist Church of Pontiac and began singing in the choir. Even as a little girl, I was impressed with the importance of telling others about Jesus. I could give my testimony as well then as I can now. During grade school I received permission to read a Bible story to my class each day. In junior high I witnessed to classmates and invited them to activities at my church. As class vice-president, I refused to participate in planning the annual dance, in order that my life would be consistent with the teachings of my church. When I entered high school, I maintained a positive outward witness and led several friends to Christ.

I loved God and the Christian way of life. I lived by the rules, but something was missing. I noticed it as I watched my older brother's life. Bob walked with the Lord consistently, uncompromisingly. I tried to be like him, but it was an imitation. I had no consistency, victory, power, joy, or peace. Doubts about my relationship with God haunted me through my early teen years. Usually I brushed them aside, talking myself into believing I was saved, deceiving my own heart.

Once during a service, I felt such conviction that I went forward seeking assurance. Knowing I had previously made a profession of faith and had lived a good life, the woman who counseled me in the prayer room said, "Rexella, you're saved. Let's pray." I had prayed all my life; I didn't need to pray right then. I needed to know if I belonged to Jesus. I left the church that night without knowing.

The Holy Spirit continued to work in my heart. At a Sunday evening service when I was sixteen, the Spirit spoke to me during my solo, "You have been singing about the Lord, but you do not know Him as a Person." Finishing the song with a burdened heart, I took a seat in the rear of the auditorium, hoping to lose myself in the crowd, beyond the Spirit's disturbing reach. Before the pastor finished his message, I slipped out of the service weeping. I wasn't saved, and I knew it. Dad saw me leave and followed me to our car.

"Oh, Dad," I sobbed. "I've made a false profession. I've fooled you and Mother, our pastor, the whole Church. But what's worse, I've fooled myself. I've known about the Lord all of my life, but I don't really know Him."

Dad might have said he was ashamed of me, or he might have tried to sweep aside my doubts. But wisely and tenderly he urged, "Rexella, be sure."

How I wanted to be sure! The following days were distressing ones until the night Bob heard me in my room, crying. His consistency had condemned me; his compassion led me to Jesus. Kneeling beside the bed with me, Bob explained the plan of salvation that I had known but had never applied to my life.

First he said I needed salvation. I had tried to live a good life, but according to Romans 3:23, "All have sinned, and come short of the glory of God." Then he explained that Christ bore our sins in His own body on the tree. I believed that, but there was one more step I had to take: I had to receive it. "But as many as received him, to them gave he power to become the sons of God, even to them that believe on his name" (John 1:12).

"I do believe," I cried. "I really do!"

"Then make a definite decision for Christ. Ask Him to come into your heart and life and be your Savior," Bob said. "And believe that if you make that decision, He will save you, cleanse you, and give you eternal life."

It was a matter of coming to a decision. I asked Jesus into my heart to be my personal Savior and Lord.

Romans 10:13 promises, "Whosoever shall call upon the name of the Lord shall be saved." What a great relief to know I was born again! No more doubts. I was sure!

Philippians 3:10 really came alive: "That I may know him, and the power of his resurrection. . . ." I knew all *about* Him, but I didn't really *know* Him until that night.

I had heard many people tell of the changes God made in their lives after they were born again. Some had backgrounds of drugs, alcohol, and such. But I had been living by the rules all along, and I wondered how I was to be changed.

Oh, how the Holy Spirit changed me! Joy filled my

soul! Peace became my daily experience! And love—I felt love greater than any I had known before, for the Lord and for those close to me. My attitudes changed. My tongue came under His control. My emotions stabilized and my life had consistency, power, and victory at last—all because I had settled life's most important question. I looked forward to a thrilling adventure with the Lord, getting to know Him better every day!

3

Love at First Sight?

When I met Jack, I was engaged to a young man who was attending Bob Jones University, where I spent a year studying music and Christian education. Since childhood I had anticipated being involved in an evangelism ministry. I had expected to team up with my preacher brother, Bob, to sing and provide piano accompaniment for his evangelistic crusades. But God had other plans.

I was home in October, 1951, to sing at the Pontiac Youth for Christ Rally. As I walked into the church, beautiful music caught my ear. I followed the melody to the basement and looked in on a handsome young accordionist.

I never had liked the accordion, but I never had heard it played so well! I listened a while as he practiced, complimented him, and went back upstairs. He never introduced himself.

I later learned that he was Jack Van Impe, a graduate of the Detroit Bible College and a friend of Bob's. Both were working for Dr. Robert Parr at Gilead Baptist Church in Detroit. Bob was announcer and soloist for Dr. Parr's weekly telecast, *The America Back to God Hour,* and Jack played the accordion.

Jack was the only son of Belgian immigrant parents who had come to America on a honeymoon trip in October of 1929, hoping to work a while and then return to their native country with enough money for a solid start. But their timing was poor; it was the beginning of the Great Depression, and their dreams melted in the heat of the sugar beet and vegetable fields of western Michigan, where they were fortunate enough to find work. After living with relatives for a year, Oscar and Louise found their own home, a rambling old house provided by the farmer they worked for in Freeport, Michigan. It was there that a son was born—destined to become a musician like his father.

After living briefly in Leipsic, Ohio, where they had buried their baby girl who died at birth, the family moved to Detroit in 1933. Oscar found work at the Plymouth Motor Car Company and began a profitable vocation as an accordionist in the Belgian beer gardens and nightclubs. The Van Impes prospered financially, but the tavern circuit was hardly the atmosphere in which to rear a child.

Years later, Oscar was convicted through the witness of a friend at work, and he turned to the Lord. Opening an old Bible given to them in Freeport (a worn book that Jack had carried around as a child and on which he had cut his teeth), Oscar invited the Lord Jesus into his heart. He was a new man, and his changed life was a witness.

Within days, Louise also gave her life to Christ. Jack, a young teen-ager, saw a change in his parents and wanted what they had. Unable to explain it well enough themselves, they sent him across the street to the Liberal Avenue Baptist Church. There he found answers to his questions, and Christ became his Savior and Lord.

Leaving the old life behind, Oscar surrendered his talent and discovered the Lord could use an accordion—two, in fact! He and Jack were a much-sought-after team for churches and evangelistic meetings. Oscar would later attend Bible college and carry the message of Christ back to Belgium.

(How grateful I am for the beautiful relationship the Lord has given to me with Dad and Mom Van Impe. They are wonderful people and so special to me!)

Jack began playing the accordion when he was five. An extremely disciplined youth, he practiced two hours daily during high school. Teaching accordion lessons helped finance his way through Bible college. His ambition was to serve the Lord in a musical ministry.

The night we met at the Youth for Christ Rally, he was billed as "Jack Van Impe, Accordionist Supreme." Having recently returned from Belgium, he was to share his testimony as well as his music.

As I crossed the platform after my testimony and song, my eyes met his.

He's so handsome! I thought. *And talented! But I shouldn't be so attracted to him. I'm engaged to someone else. Something is wrong.*

After the rally, my brother Bob introduced us. Jack asked me to go out with him for a hamburger. I wanted to, but I told him I couldn't because I was already going with someone else. A mutual friend told Jack I was engaged, and he didn't ask me out again.

I wouldn't let myself think I was attracted to Jack, but it bothered me. For weeks I prayed, "Lord, show me what is wrong."

Bob had never felt the boy I was engaged to was the one for me. I had told Bob he was wrong. My parents also did not approve of the engagement. I was not trying to be disobedient; I simply thought they were wrong. But the Lord would not let me get away from their counsel. I kept praying about it. Still feeling attracted to Jack, I knew I could not marry the other man.

On a Sunday night in December I went to Bob in tears, telling him I wanted to break the engagement. After church, he and Don drove me 250 miles through a snowstorm to Buffalo, New York. There I returned the ring to my fiancé, gently explaining that I didn't want to hurt him, but I wanted to do God's will. I was sure it was right.

Not long afterwards, Bob took me with him to sing on Dr. Parr's telecast. Jack was also on the program. His friend, Stanley Koenke, was at the studio.

"Where's your ring?" Stan asked.

"I'm not engaged any more," I replied.

He was ecstatic. "Oh, is Jack going to be happy!"

Jack asked me for a date that night. We went to church together the following Sunday and stopped at a restaurant afterward for refreshments. On the way home, he told me he loved me. I was surprised, to say the least! Then he explained that all through his teen years he had prayed for guidance in choosing a wife. When we met at the rally, he knew I was the girl God had for him. It was love at first sight!

He told me all of this on our first date. I felt very

confused. I had just broken an engagement and did not want to get serious.

"I'm sorry, Jack," I said. "I just cannot get involved for a long time." Apparently he was already sure, but I had to think and pray about it. I needed time. Thankfully, he was patient and didn't push me.

After our second date, I returned to school and Jack continued in his evangelism work. Our courtship progressed by mail. It was a difficult period for me emotionally, but when I returned home from school in March, I knew Jack was the man God meant for me. Along with the physical attraction had come a deep admiration for this man of strong principles. I knew I loved him.

On a beautiful evening in June, he proposed. We had just returned from Wednesday night prayer service. Jack remembered that in my testimony at the youth rally, I had said I would love to serve the Lord in evangelism. The living room of my parents' home was flooded with moonlight through the picture window as Jack asked sweetly and tenderly, "Would you still like to be in evangelism, only with a permanent position as my wife?"

The Lord had prepared my heart. I had no doubts. But ours was a very old-fashioned family.

"I do love you, Jack," I said, "but you will have to ask my father."

He asked, but even before he could complete his request my father, in his jovial manner, said, "If it is what I think it is—the answer is yes." My family loved him as I did!

Being an ordained minister and not wanting to bring reproach on the name of God, Jack always conducted himself as a gentleman. He didn't even kiss me in public. Driving home from a Pontiac youth rally in August, we stopped for a traffic light. It was a warm summer night and the car windows were open. Since we were to be married in a week, Jack decided it was safe to kiss me in the car. As we waited for the light to change, he took me in his arms and gave me a long, loving kiss. Suddenly we heard, "Hello, Reverend Van Impe!" It was Rev. Walter Ballaugh, pastor of First Baptist Church of Lake Orion, driving through Pontiac on his way home from Detroit. Jack almost died at the wheel! Walter has kidded him ever since.

On August 21, 1952, Jack and I were married at First Baptist Church of Pontiac, before nine hundred guests. Missing were Jack's parents, who were doing mission work in Belgium, and my brother, Bob, on the mission field in Formosa. Tears filled my eyes as we played his recording of the Lord's Prayer, and at his mission home in the Orient my brother also wept.

We wished all of our loved ones could have been there, but Mother and Dad and Don had to fill their places. Don sang and served as one of Jack's groomsmen. My younger brother was still a teen-ager, but he enjoyed our courtship days and the prospect of a brother-in-law. Not having any brothers or sisters of his own, Jack "adopted" Don and they enjoyed many times of fun together.

Our plans were to honeymoon at beautiful Mackinac Island in upper Michigan. We stopped in Traverse City on the way, as Jack was to speak at a Saturday night youth rally. We were urged to stay another night, then another. We spent our entire honeymoon at the Bible conference! Those were wonderful days in a cozy cottage on the shore of Lake Michigan, where we began our marriage and our ministry.

4

A Traveling Bride

At only nineteen, I was hardly prepared for marriage to a traveling evangelist. During our first year together there were many adjustments, many tears, and many hours on my knees. It was a time of learning for me—from the Bible and from the Holy Spirit. I had to learn who I was. That hadn't been a problem when I was at home or at school. But now, how did I fit into my husband's ministry? How could God help me help the man I loved?

At that time, books on marriage and the Christian home were not as plentiful as they are today. But I went to God's Word and found it more than adequate. Ephesians, 1 Peter, and 2 Corinthians particularly influenced my understanding of marriage and the building of our home life. I learned that submission was essential. But it was not enough to know that the Scriptures required me to be submissive to my husband. First of all I had to be submissive to God. Before I could apply such truths, I had to read and understand the Word and let Christ transform me.

Jack's life was a strong motivating factor spiritually. I saw in him many qualities of the apostle Paul: love for the Lord, strong leadership ability, compassion. He was hardworking, level-headed, stable, and practical.

I began to examine myself and ask some serious questions. If my husband is a great man, then what am I going to be? The answer came: *Rexella, you must become the woman God wants you to be.*

God used Jack's life to challenge me. He spent hours in the Word each day, leaving me with much time alone. I found it very healthy to spend that time praying and studying the Word on my own. I discovered that if I really let the Holy Spirit get hold of me, the Word would speak to me.

I had a lot of questions—no real problems, just questions. I dug into the Word and uncovered answers. I learned what I needed to know—how to be a wife, how to dress, how to react to the temperaments of other Christian workers. As I stored the Word in my heart, I noticed the Holy Spirit coming to my rescue in a variety of circumstances, bringing verses to mind to help me act and react properly. I had only to remind myself that God was in charge, working everything together for good in my life.

Early in our marriage, I realized that there is only one Person who can do something about trials and tests—the Lord. If I were to share my trials with other people, they would remember them for a lifetime. So I made it a practice never to share our problems with others; I took my heartaches to the Lord and left them there. He was the only One who could meet my needs. He always lifted the burden. Jack and I talked about things between ourselves, but due to our position in the ministry we remained very private in public.

I would not forget the truth of Proverbs 11:14, and thank God for trustworthy pastors and Christian workers in whom church members and others may safely confide. I thank Him also for allowing us to establish a counseling ministry via telephone and personal correspondence. Each year, multitudes avail themselves of this opportunity to seek and find counsel through God's Word in complete confidentiality.

People were often a disappointment to me, particularly other Christians. My family had so respected our pastor that I grew up expecting preachers to be perfect. How naive we humans can be! It would have been easier had I recognized that they are only men—God's men, to be sure, but human. We all have feet of clay! I was stunned and disillusioned when I made that discovery. One night at a prayer meeting, I knelt to pray beside a Christian worker, knowing he was an adulterer.

"Lord," I began praying silently, "give me a verse I can take for the rest of my life in evangelism so that I can work with people without becoming discouraged." He gave me some words from Hebrews 12:2: "Looking unto Jesus. . . ."

Then and there I decided, "I'm not going to look at this person or any other, only at You, Lord. People must stand before You." Since that time I have tried not to be judgmental. This does not mean that we should not recognize and confront sin, but the Bible cautions, "Judge not, that ye be not judged" (Matt 7:1). We must leave individuals and their situations with the Lord, praying that He will meet their needs as He meets ours. This makes it easier to accept people as they are.

It's unfortunate that Bible schools, seminaries, and Christian colleges don't teach good manners as a preparation for the ministry. If anyone ought to be a gentleman, a pastor or Christian worker should. He ought to know such common courtesies as standing when a lady steps to the platform and extending his hand only if she offers hers first. He ought to know how to be gentle with his children and polite to his wife, seating her at the table and opening doors for her. I have heard many men put their wives down, pretending to be funny. It was concealed hostility, meant to hurt or embarrass, and sometimes the wife left the room in tears. Many husbands and wives do this consistently. It isn't funny; it's a form of sick humor, and all of us need to avoid it.

As we traveled, I learned much from pastors' wives. The habits I saw that I didn't want to copy I categorized under "Never do that." The things I liked in their lives I mentally filed under "Always do this." The worst advice I ever received came from a missionary's wife during my first year of marriage.

"Needle your husband," she said. "Don't let him get proud."

"Don't listen to that," the Holy Spirit impressed upon me. "He is getting enough needles out there. You build him up."

I became an encourager. Whether Jack had a great message or not, I thought it was great because he not only had given the Word of God—he had given his heart and soul. I knew God could make him a great preacher. Needles from me weren't necessary. Whenever I had suggestions, even if he asked for them, I didn't share them right after his message; I always saved them for later. As wives, we must be sensitive to our husbands' moods.

For the first ten years of our ministry, we stayed in homes rather than in motels or hotels. Both Jack and I had mothers who were meticulous housekeepers. Sometimes we found ourselves in homes that were not clean. But we could not hurt anyone's feelings. Many times I scrubbed the bathtub before we used it. I must have quoted Philippians 4:13 a million times: "I can do all things through Christ which strengtheneth me." After all, we had it much better than the apostle Paul did in his ministry!

One woman showed us to our room and said, "The missionary slept there last week and he was so clean, I didn't bother to change the sheets." We couldn't hurt her by demanding clean sheets. Yet such circumstances often tried our endurance.

In one of our first meetings we stayed for a week in a home that resembled a "haunted house." It was very musty, had a bad odor, and the couple frightened me a bit. When we went to our room on the second floor, I asked, "Honey, would you push the dresser against the door?"

Jack was willing to pamper his new bride, so he did so.

"Now, push the bed in front of that."

No problem . . . until the middle of the night when Jack became ill and needed to get out in a hurry! The Lord had to deal with me in this area by giving me victory over fear.

We also ate in homes during those early years. Most of the meals were feasts a gourmet chef would have been proud of, but there were exceptions. Once I looked at my potatoes and could not see white for the flies. Leaving that home on our way to the meeting, I asked Jack to stop the car. We both got out—for the same obvious reason! Many times instead of praying, "Thank you," I prayed, "Lord, please help me to eat it."

During that first year the devil tempted me, saying, "Are you going to be on the road like this all of your life? Are you strong enough spiritually and physically?" Because of the Lord's work in my heart, I was able to pray, "I'm willing, Lord, if this is what You have for me for the rest of my life. You're enough. Having You and serving You is enough."

He more than compensated for the discomforts. Every bad memory is surrounded by a multitude of good memories of people we so quickly learned to love. Those were happy years, character-building years. God is a good Teacher; He will instruct us as we ask Him to keep us pliable and willing to be good learners. Our experiences should stimulate our spiritual growth, helping us as we in turn reach out to help others. How would we learn if all of life were easy?

Walking with Him and with "The Walking Bible" meant leaving our home behind. I had to relinquish that to God. Knowing our home was there, although it was vacant most of the time, gave me a sense of stability and security. It satisfied my "nesting instinct." But I really hardly thought of it, and that was the work of the Lord in my life: ". . . forgetting those things which are behind" (Phil. 3:13). I never wanted a lot of material possessions, but like most women I did dream about sharing a home with the man of my dreams. Yet we were on the road much of the time. I found it was enough to be serving the Lord with Jack. I was happy on the road, and when we were home we made it quality time even if it couldn't be quantity.

Do you ever feel discouraged in your ministry? You know, being a housewife and mother is the greatest ministry in the world! But sometimes you may feel like nothing more than a servant as you mop the floors, make the beds, and wash the dishes.

I remember a story about a little boy going through the family album. He found a picture of his mother, took it to her, and asked, "Mommy, is this you before you came to work for us?" I am sure that at times you have felt just that way—"I am a maid around here, nothing more!"

Let me emphasize that if your ministry is done in love, your reward will be great one day when you stand before the Lord—a reward well worth waiting for. No one can take your place—no one! You may have the satisfaction of seeing God bless your noble husband, at whose side you have stood in times of trouble and need, sharing his joys and blessings. You will receive a personal blessing as you behold your godly children, knowing that you have helped to mold their tender, young lives into strong Christian men and women. Being a godly wife and mother can be the highest calling in all the world. It may not be as glamorous as some pursuits, but it is holy and divine, and one to which you can commit yourself totally and with joy.

5

Walking With
"The Walking Bible"

When Jack gave his life to the Lord, he never dreamed of serving Him as an evangelist. Youth for Christ had featured him as an accordionist in rallies across America, and he expected to continue in that type of ministry—supplying the music for other evangelists. He actually fought the idea of preaching. When he was asked to speak, he usually took a friend along to do the preaching, while he provided the musical portion of the program. That worked for a while, until he began to feel the Lord leading him to give his testimony. Soon the Lord confirmed the call to preach. Reluctantly, but obediently, Jack allowed music to take second place. He was ordained to the ministry at twenty-one, following his graduation from Detroit Bible College.

The first years of preaching were not easy for him. He was uncomfortable before an audience without his accordion! But God was working in an amazing way. For his ordination, Jack had committed five hundred Bible verses to memory. He continued to build on that foundation, studying and memorizing two to three hours daily. Eventually, Jack would learn over eight thousand verses—the equivalent of the entire New

Testament. This accomplishment would later earn him the nickname "The Walking Bible."

Jack's memory ability is not a special gift; rather, it is the result of tremendous desire, determination, and discipline. This man who didn't want to preach has defeated intellectuals in debates all across the country because "the word of God is quick, and powerful, and sharper than any twoedged sword" (Heb. 4:12).

Storing the Word in his head and heart changed Jack's personality. As a youth he was a practical joker, forever pulling pranks on the unsuspecting. On his first trip to Belgium, Jack doused all his relatives with a water gadget concealed in a camera! In the early days of his ministry, he carried a cap gun disguised as a pen. Anyone asking Jack to autograph a Bible received a real "bang" out of it! When Jack really began to practice what the Bible teaches, however, he stopped doing what to him were childish things.

In his twenties Jack had a goal for the future: city-wide crusades. The fundamentalist camp had not sponsored many men other than Dr. Bob Jones, Sr., Dr. John R. Rice, and Dr. Jack Schuler in city-wide crusades since the days of Billy Sunday, nearly thirty years before. Jack wanted to become a city-wide evangelist not to make a name for himself, but to meet what God impressed upon his heart as a great need. In God's time, the goal would be accomplished.

The early years of our ministry found us traveling throughout America to as many as thirty-eight meetings a year, sometimes in churches with no more than seven members. Large or small, however, Jack would give all he had to make the meetings a success for Christ. It was an exciting time. More than once, a

Sunday service continued into mid-afternoon as the closing invitation stretched to three hours. Jack did not plan it this way, the Holy Spirit simply moved in an unusual way, and the entire church flocked forward to make decisions, to pray, to weep, and to praise the Lord.

After eight hundred single church crusades, the Lord again spoke to Jack's heart concerning city-wide endeavors. At that time we had fifteen hundred requests on file for single church meetings. The demand was obviously far too great for our limited ministry to supply, and Jack began considering the possibility of eight to fifty churches in an area uniting for a city-wide effort. God led the way and gave us our first united crusade when Jack was twenty-eight.

During the next twenty years we would crisscross America many times, conducting two hundred fifty united crusades, with a combined attendance exceeding ten million. We would also travel to fifty countries, with crusades scheduled in many of them. Through an interpreter, Jack preached Christ in Jerusalem. On another occasion he saw fifteen Spanish people serving at the United Nations headquarters give their lives to Him. During our crusade in the Philippines, nearly seven thousand decisions were recorded during three weeks of meetings. The local pastors, each pledging to win two hundred to Christ, followed up our visit and reported a total of seventeen thousand commitments.

Considered by many a prophet for this age, Jack is a man of strong conviction. He never ducks an issue. The Bible is clear on the subject of sin. It is black and white, not gray—and there is nothing gray about my husband. He is a lion in the pulpit, saturating his message with the Word of God. I have never tired of his preaching. In every sermon I find something for myself.

Long before the church in general accepted the principle, Jack believed that women should have an active part in church, using their talents within the biblical boundaries. He felt I had something to share, and he wanted me to share it. Through his encouragement, I determined to use my talents to the fullest and become all that God wanted me to be. I found a comfortable place in his ministry as vocalist and pianist, and also as a speaker for ladies' meetings.

The role was not as easy twenty-eight years ago as it is today. Knowing what God and Jack wanted me to do was one thing. Doing it was another. Was I brave enough?

I entered some fundamentalist churches with fear and trembling, knowing that the pastors did not allow women to say a word from their platforms. I was cautious until I won their trust. When one pastor asked me not to introduce my song, I explained that introducing the songs was part of my ministry. "Well, if it's part of your ministry, go ahead," he agreed.

"Trust me," I urged. "When I pick up the microphone, I will not take over."

I asked the Lord for wisdom in dealing with individual pastors, and God didn't let me down. At the time I did not realize it, but God was using me to help pave the way for women in fundamentalist circles to take a more active role and participate from the platform.

As our ministry grew, I felt somewhat frightened performing before such large crowds. One night the Lord gave me the same verse He had given Jeremiah:

"Be not afraid of their faces" (Jer. 1:8). After that the fear was gone. That is what the Word does when you claim its promises.

Women by the thousands have told me they appreciate the love Jack and I show toward each other. When introducing him I usually relate a humorous incident we have experienced, such as the meeting where the microphone attached to the pulpit kept falling over. Jack tried to hold it up with one hand while he preached, but with no success. Finally he exclaimed, "I wonder if someone would help me. There seems to be a screw loose in the speaker."

Sometimes Jack gets back at me. He enjoys ribbing me about being a Southerner. "When I first met Rexella, I had to teach her to wear shoes to revival meetings. I filled them with sand for two years so she would feel at home." On or off the platform we are always ourselves; no put-downs, just good-natured teasing.

I want people to feel with us as those who knew Jesus felt when they were with Him. They were not afraid. He was not haughty or austere. Every Christian should want others to feel free and at ease with him. Our witness to the world should be winsome. Others should be able to sense that the Lord is with us.

Early in our ministry I became overly concerned for those who came to Christ in our meetings. Knowing how subtly Satan could lay hold on new believers, bringing doubts and deceptions to their minds and hindering their growth and joy in serving the Lord, I wept and agonized over what might happen to them after our departure. I wanted to walk beside them in order to guard and protect them.

The Holy Spirit rebuked me, saying, "I will never

leave them nor forsake them. They are sealed for
eternity, so leave them in the hollow of My hand."

Oh, praise the Lord for His mighty everlasting work
in the lives of countless thousands! It is good to rest in
His promises and place our spiritual children in the
care of our everlasting Father.

6

Evangelist to the World

Since the first time he entered the pulpit, my husband has felt as John Wesley did, "The world is my parish." Jack wanted to saturate the world with the gospel of the Lord Jesus Christ.

Jack has always had an enormous vision for the Lord. Whenever he does something, he trusts the Lord for the entire project immediately. When he felt led to begin a radio ministry in 1972, he didn't start with just one station. If he were going to preach, he reasoned, he might as well preach to the nation. That's just what he did his first Sunday on the air—Easter Sunday when one hundred fifty stations carried the program.

But he wanted to reach out still further. It bothered him that in one U.S. city alone, forty-nine religious programs competed for a half hour on the air, while in many foreign countries there were few if any such programs.

A worldwide radio ministry was begun in 1973, taking the gospel to much of the world in English. In 1977, Trans World Radio began translating the program into foreign languages for its overseas stations. Jack's messages are now translated into more languages than any other broadcaster's using Trans World

Radio's facilities. He has made a decision to broadcast eventually in eighty-three languages, reaching billions in their native tongues and taking the Word to places behind the Iron Curtain where pastors and missionaries cannot go.

The May/June, 1980, issue of *Perhaps Today* magazine said:

Dr. Paul E. Freed, President of Trans World Radio, Chatham, New Jersey, has acclaimed Dr. Van Impe "America's first evangelist to the world." The title was given in recognition of his decision to broadcast his weekly radio program in eighty-three languages via Trans World's facilities around the globe. According to Dr. Freed, "This translation project marks the first time in history that any evangelist or religious organization has proclaimed the Gospel to all the world in the languages of the people."

From the inception of his ministry, Jack also wanted to take God's Word into the homes of America. A nationwide television ministry—perhaps his greatest vision—was launched in 1976, with hour-long, prime-time specials reaching a viewing audience of thirty million three times a year. The Lord used a young man (who has since been like a son) named Jon Byrd to encourage Jack in reaching millions by means of television. Little did Jack know that the Lord was preparing him for an even greater outreach and a drastic change in the direction of his ministry.

Having devoted thirty-three years to church and city-wide crusades, he found himself with a growing concern for those who would not come to a church or crusade meeting. In addition, increasing gasoline prices could prove a hindrance to future area-wide meetings. (In the past, some had traveled one hundred fifty miles one way to our services.)

A weekly television ministry was begun on January 1, 1980. This giant step, immediately doubling our budget, required giant faith. The response has been overwhelming. Our half-hour telecast on a growing number of stations currently draws 25,000 to 40,000 responses weekly. More than one-half million responded during the first five months. Our exciting format is quite unique in religious programming. In addition to providing the music, I frequently interview special guests (my husband calls me his "Barbara Walters in the Lord's work"). All this leads up to the message, and Jack preaches his heart out to an audience estimated to number in the millions. We believe that approximately 90 percent of the viewers do not know Jesus. Although he often follows a prophetic theme, Jack doesn't believe in being lopsided. His messages cover a variety of topics. Truly he is not ashamed of the gospel of Christ.

In order to devote our full energies to this ministry, and also to help finance it, we dropped our radio ministry in America. Our goal for the television ministry is to reach fifteen million homes weekly with the life-changing Word of God. Each year we also videotape three prime-time specials from crusade sites. New York's Carnegie Hall, Waikiki Shell in Honolulu, and the city of Anchorage, Alaska, have provided spectacular settings for three of these telecasts.

Religion in Media, a national nondenominational religious programming group based in Hollywood, presented us with an "Angel" award for outstanding contributions to prime-time television programming. It was the first time in the group's thirty-two-year history that such a national recognition award had been given. Comparable to the secular television industry's "Emmy," the Angel award was presented by RIM's executive director Mary Dorr during the taping of our 1979 Christmas special at the Grand Ole Opry House in Nashville. That special also received an Angel in 1980.

Maintaining high-caliber content and production is something my husband and I feel strongly about. We try never to do anything haphazardly. Jack's sermons, delivered without notes, are preceded by exhaustive study, and his proficiency on the accordion is the result of regular practice. Likewise, my music requires extensive production. Many hours are devoted to vocal exercise and music rehearsal. We strive to be professional in our performance but not in our persons. Our ministry has been bathed in prayer and hard work, and God has honored our efforts. Jon Byrd and Woody Robertson, our producer and director, are men sent from the Lord. Their dedication, expertise, and proficiency have been used of God to create programs that honor Him.

Being away from the crowds and working in a television studio has confirmed something we both always felt—we don't need the praise and applause of the people to have fulfillment. If the Lord would allow us to be out of what the world calls "the limelight," it wouldn't bother us at all. We could carry on a full-time ministry in solitude and still be very happy.

Financially, our work has been a struggle. The Lord has not given us bank reserves to rely on when we experience difficult periods. However, He has always spoken to His people when our needs were unusually heavy. He has never failed to supply our needs as promised.

We never have entered a new phase of ministry without much soul-searching and prayer. Jack may spend months, indeed years, thinking through an idea and seeking God's will. Then, when he senses God's time is ready, he is quick to plunge in completely. How important it is to be sensitive to the leading of the Holy Spirit! We can know God's will, but as my writer-friend Helen Hosier says, we need listening ears *and* hearing hearts. Then we need to take that giant leap of faith and be obedient.

Jack has always been a hard worker. By age eleven he was buying all of his own clothes. When he wanted a new bedroom set, his parents agreed to pay half if he could match it, and he did. At age sixteen he had three jobs: teaching accordion; selling plastic clothespins door-to-door; and working at a fruit market, putting the fruit out in the morning and taking it in at evening.

He loves to work. He spends about one hundred fifty hours per month at our crusade office in Royal Oak, Michigan. Add to this schedule fifty-two half-hour radio messages for overseas, fifty-two half-hour telecasts, one hundred twenty fund-raising banquets throughout the country, three television crusades annually, a program of review to keep up his memory work, and a writing ministry including books and a bimonthly magazine—and you will realize the tremendous amount of effort and hard work necessary to maintain this international ministry.

And you may wonder how I keep up with such a busy husband!

Jack has never been too busy for me and for our

relationship. He has his priorities straight. God gives us the energy fitted to our needs when we ask. His resources are unlimited. Tapping into the Father's supply is our privilege; indeed, it is our right as His children. God is a loving, resourceful Father who has the best interests of His children at heart. You've heard it said before, but it bears repeating because it is so true: We have not because we ask not, or because our motives are wrong. (Read James 4:2,3.)

But there is something else that needs to be emphasized. My husband takes care of himself. The Bible calls it "temple" care. Paul talks about this specifically in 1 Corinthians 3:16,17: "Know ye not that ye are the temple of God, and that the Spirit of God dwelleth in you? If any man defile the temple of God, him shall God destroy; for the temple of God is holy, which temple ye are."

To ignore this truth is to do so at our own peril. Jack and I have built into our lives a disciplined program that assures maximum health care. This includes watching what we eat and getting enough exercise and rest. It requires much discipline when we are so busy, but it can be done. We owe it to the One who so lovingly fashioned us to keep ourselves physically fit and mentally alert so that we are totally prepared for the challenges and responsibilities that come our way.

In 1968, Tennessee Temple College bestowed upon my husband an honorary doctor of divinity degree (I affectionately call him "Dr. Jack"). In 1976, Hyles-Anderson College presented Jack a doctor of humanities degree, and Baptist University of America dedicated their Chair of Evangelism to him in 1980, also giving him a doctor of theology degree. His life has exemplified 1 Peter 5:6: "Humble yourselves therefore under the mighty hand of God, that he may exalt you in due time."

If I sound like a proud wife, I must confess that I am. But I hope it is the right kind of pride. We should be proud of our husbands and their achievements; we should pat them on the back lovingly and tell them, "Honey, I am so proud of you; I am so thankful to be your wife." We win far better responses from our mates when we express our love in tangible ways like this. They need to hear and see from us that we think they are very special. You can be sure, ladies, that if you don't build up your husband's ego there are plenty of other women waiting in the wings who will. Why do so many women lose their husbands in mid-life? I believe it is because males face a mid-life identity crisis much the same way we women do.

Stop and think of the things in your husband's life that make him a unique person. The Proverbs 31 woman opened her mouth with wisdom, and in her tongue was the law of kindness (v. 26). When she looked well to the ways of her household, that must have included being complimentary to her husband and showing appreciation for his good qualities— building him up, if you please. The tender touch means so much.

Compassion is the backbone of Jack's life. My heart responds as I see him shake off exhaustion to enfold a child in his arms, patiently answering his questions about Jesus. Even now, he is the last one to leave the auditorium whenever we have meetings. Somehow I think he feels Jesus Christ would be the last one to leave.

My heart goes out to you women with problem marriages. I have encountered you in meetings across

America and in our trips abroad. My prayers include you and your circumstances, the things you have confided to me. My prayer is that even now you will be strengthened and encouraged, and that you will seek ways to change your marital relationship, with God's help. It can be done. Jesus never gave up on those whom others considered hopeless, and we should strive to be like Him.

7

Safe
in God's Will

The location was Kansas City, Missouri; the year, 1972. Policemen entered the auditorium where our crusade meeting was in progress. An officer came to the platform and whispered a message to Jack. I sensed he was praying for a moment. Then he calmly announced to the audience of several thousand, "Nothing is going to happen tonight, so please don't be disturbed. We have had a threat on our lives. That is why the police have come, but don't let that upset you. Now my wife is going to sing."

My husband's life was in danger, and he expected me to sing! Still, the Lord had prepared me, and I stood to share my confidence: "Isn't it wonderful how God prepares us for everything in life? I believe the Lord is going to protect my husband. Nobody is going to hurt him unless it is God's perfect will." Then I sang the song I had been practicing that afternoon—"God knows all about tomorrow and He holds today in His hand."

Later, the police discovered that a section of the air conditioning system had been removed, apparently part of the assassination plan. Just minutes before the services had begun, a man had rushed up to Jack urging him to come to the prayer room immediately.

When told he must wait until after the meeting, the man had gone away cursing. We believe that having Jack go to the prayer room was to have been the key move in the narcotics-related plot involving three men. Several local drug pushers had been converted during the crusade, disrupting the narcotics trade. We were provided police protection for the next forty-eight hours—and divine protection indefinitely!

Satan has relentlessly attacked our ministry. He never gives up. He has tried to take our lives. Through storms, illnesses, accidents, and vandalism he has tried to prevent our television specials. But we have been safe in God's will. We have not suffered as the apostle Paul did, but we identify with his trials and triumphs summarized in 2 Corinthians 4:8–10: "We are troubled on every side, yet not distressed; we are perplexed, but not in despair; Persecuted, but not forsaken; cast down, but not destroyed; Always bearing about in the body the dying of the Lord Jesus, that the life also of Jesus might be made manifest in our body."

Jack and I believe that Satan's vicious assaults on ministries that are faithfully preaching the Word will continue at an accelerated pace. Satan's time is short. And he already has the secular world, so why waste time on them! The enemy's onslaughts will be directed with greater fervor toward Christians, Christian families, the church that holds steadfastly to the Bible, and radio and television ministries that introduce listeners and viewers to the God of our salvation and His Son.

The year was 1976; the city was Philadelphia. We were honored to be chosen as the evangelistic team for the Bicentennial crusade in this historic city. News-

papers and magazines across the nation carried re-
ports of the violence planned by Communists and
militant supporters to disrupt America's birthday
celebration. My husband had received threatening
letters indicating the militants wanted him "out of the
way." As we left for Philadelphia his heart was heavy,
knowing he might not return, yet confident he was in
the Lord's will. In spite of this, we were not consumed
by fear.

Our first night in Philadelphia, three truckloads of
militants arrived at the hotel where we were staying
and marched past with the clenched-fist salute of the
Communist party. Radicals were interviewed on television and boldly boasted their plans to dynamite the
city July 4. Fear was in the air. The enemy of our souls
was having a heyday. As a result, the millions expected to converge on the city for the Bicentennial
festivities stayed away. Fifty of the churches sponsor-
ing our crusade decided to conduct their own services
to avoid any violence.

At the crusade, guards were assigned to our platform. Expecting an assassination attempt, they in-
sisted that Jack wear a bulletproof vest. He felt so
handicapped by it the first night that he prayed and
concluded it was a lack of faith to wear the vest. He
discarded it, and from that moment he was filled with
perfect peace. We quoted Romans 8:28 and trusted the
Lord. With large crowds each night and a local attendance of 40,000 for the week, we feel the gospel made
an impact on the city. We praise the Lord for His
divine protection.

In spite of the enemy's clever schemes, Jack has
never missed a night of meetings in more than thirty-
three years. Several years ago, a siege of sciatica left

him temporarily unable to walk, but he refused to cancel a crusade. Ignoring the pain, he crawled to the car, pulled himself in, and drove to Hammond, Indiana. He was carried into the church and placed in a chair so that he could play the accordion and preach. Afterward he was carried back to the car. This continued for the entire crusade. Two toes on his left foot are numb as a result of this experience, but Satan did not defeat him!

In twenty-eight years I have missed only eight weeks, due to surgery. But I also know what it is to serve in sickness. For most of the first twelve years of our ministry, I was so physically weak that there were nights I scarcely had the strength to sing. Satan waged some mighty battles, but he never won the war.

8

Pain:
A Way of Life

My "thorn in the flesh" is my health. Through illness Satan tried to ruin my life. He could have destroyed my marriage and my ministry, but I was determined he was not going to do this!

As a young bride I wanted children, lots of little accordion players! In the first few years of marriage, however, I realized I was having a problem. I had been to many doctors before the Lord led me to a fine gynecologist in Detroit. He correctly diagnosed the cause of a problem that had afflicted me as far back as my high school days, and strongly recommended a hysterectomy. But since that would eliminate forever the possibility of having a baby, I determined not to have it done.

That decision could have cost my life.

Depending on the strength of the Lord, I carried on, relying heavily upon His promise, "As thy days, so shall thy strength be" (Deut. 33:25). When the pain kept me in bed all day, Jack would kneel by the bed and pray for the pain to subside so that I could sing at the crusade. Following the services I would go back to bed. The next day would be the same. No one else knew what I was going through, not even my family.

During this period I was greatly comforted by a

thought in Charles Spurgeon's devotional book, *Morning and Evening.* He states, "Wisdom hangs up the thermometer at the furnace mouth, and regulates the heat." The Lord gave me strength to go on. His grace enabled me to endure without complaining.

Satan seemed to take pride in trying to hurt me physically. But one of the strengths of my temperament is determination. I simply will not give up. By the grace of God that quality has taken me through seemingly insurmountable circumstances.

I became accustomed to pain. I learned to bear pain almost as a way of life. Yet the joy of the Lord never left me during those years of hoping. In 1958, surgery was performed in an effort to improve the possibility of my having children, but the condition did not improve. I identified with Hannah's weeping for a child. I couldn't understand the reason I was not allowed to have a baby. "Is it because I wouldn't be a good mother?" I asked the Lord. I made Him promises: "I'll keep serving You. I'll keep traveling with Jack. I'll take the children with me."

But always I had to say, "More than that, I want Your will." In my flesh I didn't want to say it, but with the help of the Spirit I could pray, "Thy will be done."

My answer came in 1967. I suffered a severe attack during a concert—an extreme case of endometriosis. I couldn't walk. My life was in danger. A hysterectomy would have to be performed.

Once again the Lord spoke to me through the wisdom of my brother Bob. At the time he was serving as pastor of our home church after being forced to leave Viet Nam during the height of the war. (The Viet Cong had tried many times to kill him for his preaching.) When our beloved minister, Dr. H. H. Savage, retired after thirty-eight years, Bob was called to pastor First Baptist Church of Pontiac, Michigan, where we had grown up.

"Rexella," he said to me one day, "you don't have to smoke to destroy the temple of the Holy Spirit."

I put a fleece before the Lord: "If in one year I do not have a child, I will have the surgery." I left it with the Lord and waited. My physical problems worsened.

Jack urged me to have surgery for my health's sake, and I finally agreed. God gave me peace. Apparently, it was not His will for us to have children. He had something else for us.

Adopting a child had been considered, but we were convinced it was not God's will for us. We had prayed it through long ago and settled the matter when a phone call came one night. Someone offered us a child to adopt. I wanted the child, but I knew in my heart it was not God's will. It took a good deal of strength from the Lord to enable me to say, "I am sorry, but we have prayed it through and we just cannot adopt a child."

It was the hardest thing I ever had to do. I cried. That is normal. Tears are God's tranquilizer. I prayed for that child, that God would provide a mother to love and nurture the little one and that the child would become all that God wants her or him to be. I adopted that baby in my heart!

I don't allow myself to think, "If I had a child . . ." The Holy Spirit has filled my life with other joys. He set us apart for a special ministry. In many ways Jack is very strong, but in other ways he is dependent upon the strength God has given me. If it had been necessary for Jack to travel alone, evangelism would have been a very lonely and difficult life for him. Certainly the Lord could have arranged other circumstances—a co-evangelist, for example. But I believe His plan was for me to travel with him. He has given us thousands upon thousands of spiritual children to compensate for the little ones we never had.

Although Jack also wanted children, he never felt we had to have children in order to have a home and be a family. The Lord didn't create Adam and Eve—and children. The first home belonged to Adam and Eve alone. God later gave them children to populate the earth and to add joy to their home. Our home has been complete even though we have no children. Still, it was the most difficult area in which God has dealt with me. To accept His will, I first had to be convinced His will was best. Once I accepted that, I rejoiced in what my life could be.

Most women want children. Some have careers and wish to accomplish something on their own before starting families. I see nothing wrong with that. God has timing. Just as there is order to everything, there is a time for everything. The only way we can know the Lord's will is through studying His Word, committing our needs and desires to Him in prayer, and then waiting patiently.

Every time I prayed about a family, God would say to me in my inner spirit, "I have something better for you." I was never bitter, for which I give God the glory. I long for other childless women to know that God is not taking anything away from them or trying to hurt them. He has something better. What could be better than children? Only having His will.

9

Through
the Deep Waters

Jack and I had been together throughout most of his ministry, in church and city-wide crusades, one-night rallies, and radio and television appearances that totaled fifteen thousand. In all of this we were a team, united in marriage and ministry, wading through many deep waters.

In August of 1979, we were together at the edge of eternity in Belgium.

A city bus slammed into our car. Jack gripped the steering wheel, but the impact threw him onto the seat, unconscious. Moments later he came to himself—bruised, bleeding, and emotionally shaken. He rushed to my side, finding me lying on the street in a pool of blood and in shock. Oblivious to the curious crowd that gathered, he cradled me in his arms as he wept and prayed, "Lord, must it end this way? Don't let it happen! Please work a miracle!"

I was unconscious, unable to think or move. One thing I knew . . . I was dying. But I was not frightened. Suspended in the sweetest peace, I was almost in the presence of the Lord. Then, suddenly, I was pulled back from going over. A man grasped my wrist.

"Don't move her," he said with authority. "She will be all right." He spread a blanket over me. Then, as mysteriously as he had appeared, he was gone. The moment he spoke, my mind began to clear. I knew that I would live.

Then I was aware of pain—intense pain.

"Lord, help me!" was all I could think to pray.

Jack kept repeating, "I'm sorry . . . I'm sorry . . ." Because he was driving he felt responsible, although he was not at fault and could not have averted the accident. I was reassured to know he was not badly hurt.

An ambulance rushed us to the hospital. It was a modern facility in downtown Brussels, but it was unsophisticated by American standards. Treatment was not administered with the sympathy and kindness we are accustomed to in our country. No gown was provided when my outer garments were cut away, leaving me scantily clothed and nearly stripped of dignity. Yet I was grateful to be alive.

Soon, X-rays revealed that I had a broken collarbone, numerous cuts and bruises, and fragments of glass embedded in many parts of my body. The doctor spent four hours removing glass from my legs, head, and ears. God had divinely and miraculously spared my face and eyes, for which I am very grateful.

Because of my head injury I was unable to receive any pain medication for eighteen hours. They said that if the bleeding from my head wound did not stop during the night, they would have to shave my head in order to suture the extreme abrasion. My wonderful husband was by my side every minute of that entire night to pray with me, comfort me, and talk with me. We asked God for a miracle, and again He gave us one. By morning the bleeding had stopped.

Neither of us slept during that long, unforgettable

night. We talked about why it had happened. I felt a kinship to Job. God had allowed Satan to test us, but not to destroy us or our ministry. He allowed the test to go only so far. I knew my Father was in control and my Savior was not leaving me alone. Indeed, I knew He was walking through this time with me.

I must not fail Him, I thought.

He reminded me of the promise, "And we know that all things work together for good to them that love God, to them who are the called according to His purpose" (Rom. 8:28). All things working together, not only for His glory but also for my good!

Jack spent the next forty-eight hours trying to get the doctors to release me for our trip back to the States. British Airways agreed to fly us and graciously provided wheelchair and ambulance service all the way to Detroit. Again the providential hand of our Lord reached out, and every detail was arranged. The trip home was painfully long, and only because of 2 Timothy 4:17 did I manage to endure: "Notwithstanding the Lord stood with me, and strengthened me."

We had not notified our parents of the accident. When they saw me come from the plane in a wheelchair, they didn't know what to think. When we came close enough for them to see my bruises and my hair still matted with blood, they almost fainted. Cancelling a planned vacation, Mother and Dad stayed with us for two weeks, enabling me to recuperate at home while Jack continued his work.

For three months I received extensive medical treatment and stringent therapy. A brace was used to set the collarbone. No X-rays had been made of the rib area in Belgium and now I learned how fortunate I was that my lungs had not been punctured. The X-rays taken at home revealed that I had two fractured ribs; one easily could have damaged my lungs.

When my arm came out of the brace after about eight weeks, it was almost immobile. Adhesions had formed as the damaged muscles and tendons in the crushed shoulder had healed. Therapy twice weekly did not improve function. Doctors recommended surgery, which might involve rebreaking the bone. They were convinced that without surgery, I had only a fifty-fifty chance of lifting my arm higher than shoulder level.

The therapist showed Jack how to do the therapy so that I could continue while we vacationed in Florida. Through performing the exercise several times a day, Jack literally tore up those adhesions. It was very painful and I couldn't keep back the tears. But the result was a miracle—the arm rebuilt itself. I began treatments with our chiropractor for whiplash and discovered that he was also helping my arm in an unbelievable way. I have complete use of it now, and experience pain only when exercising to keep it limber. The healing without surgery is nothing short of a miracle.

Five weeks after the accident, I taped four weekly television programs and the special telecast of the Nashville crusade, which was to be shown nationwide at Christmas. The Lord gave me clearness of mind even under heavy medication, but the schedule was too much. I almost collapsed. I was forced to slow down for a few more weeks. He reminded me of a lesson learned years before—I must walk one step at a time, totally dependent upon Him. I had to relearn that.

He reinforced another lesson—never worry. At the

time of the accident I was worried about two things: finances for the expanded television ministry, and my ability to work effectively in this outreach. The Lord took that fear from me. I promised Him that with His help, I would try to stop worrying and trust Him as never before. I had trusted Him before, but now I have a joyful trust that the devil can never take from me. The pain was worth it.

Through the accident God also worked in Jack's life, giving him perfect assurance that while we may endure trials and testings, nothing can stop us until God's final call comes. Satan did his best to stop our ministry. The accident was his trump card. But he was no match for our mighty God!

Jack and I have claimed 2 Corinthians 4:17, 18: "For our light affliction, which is but for a moment, worketh for us a far more exceeding and eternal weight of glory; While we look not at the things which are seen, but at the things which are not seen: for the things which are seen are temporal; but the things which are not seen are eternal."

There was no explanation for the mysterious stranger. I believe he was an angel sent by God to deliver me from the hand of Satan. "Are [angels] not all ministering spirits, sent forth to minister for them who shall be heirs of salvation?" (Heb. 1:14). The cosmos is filled with angels who camp round about us, oftentimes to deliver us from impending danger. Guardian angels are instruments of our great God, dispensing His love and tender, solicitous watch care!

I discovered what it is like to arrive at that moment when you may die, and I learned that the unknown is not a fearful thing. Even for Christians, the thought of that valley of death we each must pass through one day is a little frightening. I wish I could describe the peace I felt and proclaim from a mountaintop to believers everywhere: "Don't be afraid!" At the moment of departure, He will be there to give us peace and sustain our heart. What a comfort to know that we are the Lord's most prized possessions, and that He will not allow us to go through the transition from this life to the next in fear. I know the significance of what David said: "Yea, though I walk through the valley of the shadow of death, I will fear no evil: for thou art with me" (Ps. 23:4).

Deep waters—everyone passes through them. Long ago I learned that great blessing can come as a result of these experiences. And what a promise we have! "When thou passest through the waters, I will be with thee; and through the rivers, they shall not overflow thee . . . For I am the LORD thy God, the Holy One of Israel, thy Savior" (Is. 43:2,3). I can now look back on the accident with rejoicing and praise—rejoicing in the Lord's protection and love in bringing us through this trial, and praise that He counted us worthy to be put to the test. Satan surely meant it for evil, but God meant it for good.

10

Could We Talk Heart to Heart?

I wish that you were sitting here in my living room with me and that we could talk woman to woman, friend to friend. I wish we could share our lives—the hurts and the happiness. You know a good deal about me now, but I know so little of you—only that you are a woman; perhaps a wife, perhaps a mother, perhaps a single person.

If we could talk, what would you say to me? Would it be a superficial conversation, skimming lightly over topics of no real interest to either of us? Or could we lay aside the masks all of us wear from time to time and share as sisters? You might tell me of the tempers that flared at breakfast and the ache in your heart during the hours you waited for the family to return so you could say, "I'm sorry." You might tell me of that "I-might-as-well-give-up" feeling as day after day you face the same unmade beds, dirty dishes, piles of laundry, appointments, ringing phones, and door-bells with no time even to make yourself look pretty, let alone feel pretty.

You might tell me of the pressures of your job away from home, the financial problems that are forcing you to work, or the guilt you feel simply because you want to work. You might tell me of your son who is in trouble with the law, or who is destroying his life with drugs or alcohol, and the overwhelming sense of failure that accuses you. Perhaps you would tell me of your daughter, still a child herself, who is now with child and without a husband.

If we could talk, you might tell me of the disappointment of having everything in life but what you wanted most—precious children. You could tell me of the bitterness of growing old, never having found the "right man," or the one you did find having deserted you. You could tell me of the habit that enslaves you and from which, though you hate it, you cannot break free. You might even tell me of the thoughts buried so deep within that you're afraid to let yourself consider them. You might tell me of past guilt that still haunts you and makes your life a living grave.

Oh, you may tell me! Many women have!

I hope you would not say, "What do you know? Your life reads like a fairy tale. You can't relate to me!" Please! Don't feel that way! My hurt may be different, but it is hurt just the same. And what I have to give is not an invisible bandage for bleeding wounds that will not heal. Would you let me speak to you for just a moment—heart to heart?

God loves *you*, just as you are. He loves you deep down inside where you don't even like yourself. He knows all your weaknesses—the hatefulness, the anger, the bitterness, the impatience, the wickedness, the doubt, the turmoil. You don't have to pretend anything. Honest! He knows it all, but still He loves you! And even more than you want it yourself, He wants to fill your life with love, joy, peace, patience, gentleness, goodness, faith, meekness, and self-control (see Gal. 5:22,23). This wonderful fruit is produced by His Spirit living inside believers and controlling their lives. But first you must receive His Spirit by being born again.

Jesus said, "Except a man be born again, he cannot see the kingdom of God" (John 3:3). What does it mean to be "born again"? When we are born physically, we receive our parents' nature; we are a new generation. When we are born spiritually—into God's family—we receive Christ's nature; we are a new creation (2 Cor. 5:17).

Let me explain it this way: I have a cat named Fenica (Flemish for Josephine), and I love her! I talk to her all the time. Yet, in a real sense, we cannot communicate. The reason is simple—I have a human nature, and Fenica has a cat nature. If, however, I could somehow take upon myself Fenica's nature, and implant in her my nature, we could really communicate!

God is confronted with somewhat the same problem in respect to man. In order for our salvation to be secured, His Son, Jesus Christ, took upon Himself human nature (in Mary's womb), yet without interfering with His divine nature. Thus, He became as one of us, except for sin. Conversely, the moment we come into union with Christ as Savior, we become "partakers of the divine nature" (2 Pet. 1:4). We do not become God, but we are made a new creation (2 Cor. 5:17) through the forgiveness of our sin and receipt of His nature by the implanting of His Holy Spirit within us. In short, we become a child of God.

This is what the new birth is all about—a change in the nature of our heart. We can now communicate with God, and He can communicate with us through the power of the Holy Spirit.

You ask, "How does all of this happen?" Simply by

turning from our sin and turning to Christ, asking Him to come into our heart and rule our life (Rom. 10:9,10,13). Jesus Himself said, "Behold I stand at the door and knock: if any man hear my voice and open the door, I will come in to him and will sup [communicate] with him, and he with me" (Rev. 3:20). You don't have to live with uncertainty, as I once did, empty and afraid on the inside, wondering whether you are good enough for heaven or bad enough for hell. Inviting Jesus into your heart is the first step you must take if your life is to experience this glorious change.

Perhaps you have already received Christ as Savior but are living in defeat because sin has hidden God's face from you. In this case, you need to confess your sin and claim the promise of 1 John 1:9: "If we confess our sins, He is faithful and just to forgive us our sins, and to cleanse us from all unrighteousness."

Once you have accepted Christ and obtained the forgiveness of sin, a direct line of communication is established between you and God. It is somewhat like talking to someone over the telephone. You cannot see the other person, but he or she is obviously real and there on the other end of the line talking with you. The telephone is an electronic miracle; Christianity is a divine miracle. God communicates with every believer through His Word, through prayer, and through speaking to the heart. To neglect any one of these avenues of communication is to stunt one's spiritual growth.

The Christian life is a growth process. Each day you will grow stronger in faith and reliance upon God. As you abandon your will to do His, the Spirit will control your life and produce the refreshing fruit listed in

Galatians 5—love, joy, peace, patience, gentleness, goodness, faith, meekness and self-control. Doesn't that sound like the good life you've been searching for?

I remember a young lady who almost lost everything before she found Christ. After I had finished singing in a crusade meeting, she motioned that she would like to talk with me. She was radiant with the love of the Lord and that unmistakable glow of inner peace. She began her story by thanking me for a song I had sung the last time we were in that area.

Then, solemnly, she said, "Do you see my wrists? These scars are the result of my trying to take my life. I had tried everything imaginable to find peace of mind and heart. Finally, in despair, I attempted suicide. After being released from the hospital, I came to hear your husband preach. Before he spoke that night, you sang a song entitled, 'Please Remember, God Loves You!' That was the beginning of the answer I had been searching for—God's love! Then your husband preached and my heart responded to the message of hope and Christ. Thank you for helping show me the way, the only way to real peace and joy, and my greatest earthly treasure—eternal life!"

Please remember that God loves you, too! He wants to transform your life. You *cannot* remain the same once the Holy Spirit comes into your life. He *will* make a difference in your heart and in your home. Will you let Him do this—right now?

I do wish we could talk face to face. This conversation seems so one-sided! But there is much more I want to share with you. Let me continue with some more thoughts about you—a very special woman.

11

Please Look a Little Deeper

"Man looketh on the outward appearance, but the Lord looketh on the heart" (1 Sam. 16:7).

Have you noticed that people often reflect only on the second half of that sentence, overlooking the first part? Man *does* look on the outward appearance, and it's important to know that! The first impression you convey is based on how you look. People judge you from the first moment they look at you. As Christians, we need to be our best and to look our best at all times, for the glory of the Lord.

A woman's entire person should reflect her discretion and good taste. She should dress fashionably, as long as the style does not violate what the Bible teaches. Our guideline should be 1 Timothy 2:9,10. We are to dress modestly and in good taste. Our appearance should not be gaudy and, certainly, not slovenly. Remember, your appearance reflects your attitude.

Careful wardrobe planning can also result in considerable financial savings. (Some women buy pink shoes and discover they have nothing to wear with them. What a waste!) Choose items you can use, and don't be afraid to invest in quality goods. They may be a little more expensive, but they will last longer. In the long run, you will save money and feel good about the way you look.

I did not come from a wealthy home, but we always wore quality clothing. My parents taught me to select one good dress instead of five inferior ones. Suits have always been practical for me; with a change of blouses, a suit can become a whole new outfit. However, for platform appearances I prefer the softer look of a flowing dress. Above all, I don't want what I wear to distract the audience from the message of my song.

I choose something bright when Jack wears black. At other times I select a color that blends with what he is wearing. It isn't necessary that we always match, but in a room full of people I think it is nice to be able to identify the man and woman who belong to each other. I never want Jack to be concerned with my appearance for one minute; that should be the least of his worries. I dress to please him, and to please the Lord. For me, that is enough.

Does your clothing flatter your figure? I have a weight problem; my trouble is keeping pounds! At my height (five-feet-five) I feel my best at 103 pounds. I lose weight and vitality if I miss sleep (seven hours a night) and fail to pace myself. I've learned that I cannot keep up with my husband!

Losing pounds may be your problem. "Thin" seems to be the rule of the day. But not every woman is going to be thin. Many women find it difficult to lose weight. You do not have to be thin to be attractive. However, if gluttony is a besetting sin, then please do something about it. Seek medical help if necessary. Try. But *don't* become depressed.

Whatever your weight, exercise is important. I follow a little routine to keep firm. You'll feel better if you have one, too, even if you can spare only ten minutes a day. Make it something fun, like walking, bicycling, or jogging. You won't regret devoting this time to yourself.

Do all that you can to bring out your natural beauty. Cosmetics work wonders! Years ago I learned to apply makeup so that my face would not mirror my poor health. Accentuate the positive; highlight your good points. Above all, give attention to your eyes. Take care that they show the joy of the Lord. Whatever you are inside will show through your eyes.

When I was young I complained to my mother about how bad I looked. She turned to 1 Peter 3:3,4: "Let it not be that outward adorning of plaiting the hair, and of wearing of gold, or of putting on of apparel; But let it be the hidden man of the heart, in that which is not corruptible, even the ornament of a meek and quiet spirit, which is in the sight of God of great price." This does not dismiss the outward appearance as unimportant, but the inner self must come through stronger than anything else.

May I also add that verse 3 does not prohibit the use of cosmetics or jewelry or hair styling. Otherwise, the Lord would also be against the wearing of clothes! It only means to be careful not to allow the outward appearance to take precedence over the inward person. My husband has often said, "If the barn needs a little paint, paint it!"

One woman who attended a crusade said to me, "I wasn't going to come tonight because you wear makeup."

"Please look a little deeper," I urged.

The inward person and the outward person—we cannot neglect either.

How are you dressed spiritually? Colossians 3:8–10 may give you a clue. "But now ye also put off all these; anger, wrath, malice, blasphemy, filthy communication out of your mouth. Lie not one to another, seeing that ye have put off the old man with his deeds; And have put on the new man, which is renewed in knowledge after the image of him that created him."

If you look a little deeper, will you find the closet of your heart needs attention?

12

The Virtuous Woman

"Who can find a virtuous woman? For her price is far above rubies."

With that introduction, the godly woman is described in Proverbs 31:10–31:

The heart of her husband doth safely trust in her, so that he shall have no need of spoil.

She will do him good and not evil all the days of her life.

She seeketh wool, and flax, and worketh willingly with her hands.

She is like the merchants' ships; she bringeth her food from afar.

She riseth also while it is yet night, and giveth meat to her household, and a portion to her maidens.

She considereth a field, and buyeth it: with the fruit of her hands she planteth a vineyard.

She girdeth her loins with strength, and strengtheneth her arms.

She perceiveth that her merchandise is good: her candle goeth not out by night.

She layeth her hands to the spindle, and her hands hold the distaff.

She stretcheth out her hand to the poor; yea, she reacheth forth her hands to the needy.

She is not afraid of the snow for her household: for all her household are clothed with scarlet.

She maketh herself coverings of tapestry; her clothing is silk and purple.

Her husband is known in the gates, when he sitteth among the elders of the land.

She maketh fine linen, and selleth it; and delivereth girdles unto the merchant.

Strength and honor are her clothing; and she shall rejoice in time to come.

She openeth her mouth with wisdom; and in her tongue is the law of kindness.

She looketh well to the ways of her household, and eateth not the bread of idleness.

Her children arise up, and call her blessed; her husband also, and he praiseth her.

Many daughters have done virtuously, but thou excellest them all.

Favor is deceitful, and beauty is vain: but a woman that feareth the LORD, she shall be praised.

Give her of the fruit of her hands; and let her own works praise her in the gates.

Did you notice that this gracious woman is devoted to her family and home? Her "fulfillment" is found in fulfilling the purpose for which she was created. She is a woman of strength, honor, wisdom, and kindness. Her husband, her children, and the community reward her devotion with praise. Doesn't she seem to be the ideal woman? Faithful wife. Devoted mother. Diligent homemaker. Loyal friend. Do you know one like her? I do.

My mother is like the woman of Proverbs 31. In my view, she has been the perfect mother. Always gentle, she never lashed out at us in anger. I could confide in her and know that she would understand and would keep my confidence. She taught me by example all of the good qualities of Christian character. Her love and wisdom indelibly marked my life.

I shall never forget the day I came to her as a teen-ager to confess a disobedient deed. Mother had told me very definitely not to do it, but I had decided to do it anyway. The Lord would not let me live with that secret. Mother was lying down one afternoon (a very rare thing for her, as she was a combined Mary and Martha, worshiping the Lord and serving Him fervently), and I thought this would be an opportune time to confess.

"Mother," I said, kneeling by her bed. "I have lived with something for several months now and I must confess it to you. Do you recall that you told me not to _____? I did it anyway."

She looked at me and a tear rolled down her cheek. Gently putting her hand on my face, she said, "Oh, Rexella, I'm sorry you had to bear that burden all alone for so long."

Instead of flaring up in anger, she showed perfect compassion, love, and understanding. That kind of wisdom must come from the Lord. "If any of you lack wisdom, let him ask of God, that giveth to all men liberally" (James 1:5).

My mother asked and received liberally! What a beautiful example she has been of the virtuous woman!

The Lord also blessed my life with two godly grandmothers. Both were homemakers supreme! Florida Hodge, my mother's mother, reared seven children. My father's mother, Hettie Shelton, had a brood of eight. They were both fantastic about providing for their families, and neither was ever too busy for me. My best memories of them are of their love.

Grandma Hodge loved to sew. When I was a little girl, she made my whole wardrobe. I suppose she made a hundred colorful quilts in her lifetime. She gave most of them away to her children, grandchildren, relatives, and friends. She loved and cared for everyone, and you could count on her to be there if you were ill—food in hand. She was always the first to respond. She was also one of the most unselfish persons I've ever known and, like my mother, so understanding. In junior high I had some physical problems and often did not feel well. Many afternoons I went to her nearby home directly from school.

"Come in and lie down," she'd smile. "Now talk to me about it." She was such a comfort. We had some precious times of prayer together.

I shall never forget the day she taught me to spell my first word. I was about five years old and was watching her make an apple pie. She was always busy, but never too busy for a five-year-old granddaughter.

"When I finish," she said, "we'll go down to the dime store and have a banana split."

"How do you spell that?" I wanted to know.

In the flour on the counter she wrote, "banana." Then she erased it.

"Now you try it."

I still remember writing "banana" with my finger in the flour! And when the pie was finished, we went to the dime store for that banana split! I trusted my grandmothers because they always did what they promised.

Grandma Shelton stood five-feet-ten. She would pick me up and hug and shake me like a rag doll, saying, "I love you!" She sang, hummed, and whistled her way through life. A woman of great compassion, she genuinely cared about people and always found time to visit those who needed her. She crocheted beautiful afghans for family and friends. Her yard was a profusion of flowers, and a silent sign of welcome seemed to hang above her door. There was always room for more at her big table, spread with a feast of fried chicken and homemade cornbread. Hymns from her harmonica filled the quiet evenings.

Life gave her many physical ailments, but Grandma Shelton displayed the Christian virtue of longsuffering, never complaining. One leg was amputated due to diabetes, but she never lost her joy in the Lord. Upon receiving a pair of stockings for Christmas, she exclaimed, "Isn't the Lord wonderful! They will last twice as long now!" Later she lost the other leg. When I walked into her hospital room and realized that she would never be a physically strong person and stand again, it nearly broke my heart. I knelt by her wheelchair and started to cry. She stopped me. "Don't you waste one tear on me because I am going to be walking up *there*!"

Before she went home to heaven I received this beautiful note.

Dear Rexella,
I am really glad to leave this bunch of children and grandchildren in the hands of the Lord. When I am gone, you can know that I am with Him. I didn't do much, but with the help of the Lord I did all I could do.
All my love,
Grandma.

When Grandma died, Jack and I were in Hawaii for a crusade. Knowing that we could not come home, my father didn't call until we arrived in Florida for our next meeting. That night I felt compelled by the Holy

Spirit to get out of bed and pray. I don't know everything about heaven, but believing that God gives us the desires of our heart, I prayed, "Lord, give Grandma a message for me. Just tell her 'thank you.' "

My life has been so enriched by these virtuous women. Let me ask you: What memories are you leaving your children and grandchildren?

13

Love and Iron in the Spine

"Love your husband. It will put iron in his spine." This is the best advice I ever received—and the best I can give. I've made it my philosophy.

"I don't love my husband any more," confided a troubled wife in Pennsylvania following a morning service. In the back of the auditorium, a young man with two children waited.

"Is that your husband?" I guessed correctly. She then related a story I'd heard a thousand times in my travels across the country. A wife becomes bogged down at home with two small children. Her husband doesn't try to understand her feelings. Bitterness builds upon bitterness, and soon the marriage is destined for divorce.

"I don't love my husband any more." This woman's story began the same way. But this time it was a close friend confessing that she had fallen in love with her boss. Working together day after day had led to a physical attraction, and then to an intimate relationship. Another marriage was destined for divorce.

Currently, almost one out of two marriages in the United States ends in divorce. In some states, the number of divorces exceeds the number of marriages. What can be done about this shocking trend?

I believe everything under God's heaven should be done to prevent divorce. The Lord leaves room for divorce only in the matter of infidelity—proven adultery, not suspicions or bitterness.

God, who is the same yesterday, today, and forever, has not changed His mind. Marriage is still sacred. Adultery is still sinful. Sin is still punished.

My heart breaks when I realize that churches abound with unsaved men and women who are living immoral lives. King David committed adultery, but he later wept over his sin. Today, people return home from such sinful activity and sleep well—an indication that they are not genuinely born again. An unsaved person can live in sin and never be troubled. A saved person can commit the act a second time, but he is bound to weep harder. God will deal with him.

If you are involved in an adulterous relationship, be enough of a Christian woman to take control of your emotions. You must end the relationship. If he's your boss, ask for a transfer or quit your job and seek employment elsewhere. You cannot continue the relationship under any circumstances.

Ask the Lord to give you a greater love for your husband. Should you tell him? Most counselors and theologians agree that if it is believed the husband could not cope with this, it is better to leave it with the Lord. It will surely hurt your husband and he might not be able to forgive or forget. David said, "Against thee, thee only, have I sinned, and done this evil in thy sight" (Ps. 51:4). Once your sin is confessed and God has cleansed you, removing all guilt, go and sin no more. (Chapter 22 discusses more about guilt.)

With the Lord's help, your marriage can be saved. You must be willing to try. Marriage is not a matter of simply saying "I do" and living the rest of your life solely on that commitment. The marriage relationship requires work day by day in order to grow stronger.

Every home has a barometer that alerts us to approaching storms. I call it the "love level." Love for your husband begins at a certain level, and then it should grow, just as one's love for God starts at salvation and should grow deeper with each passing year. "Nevertheless I have somewhat against thee," said the Lord to the church at Ephesus, "because thou hast left thy first love" (Rev. 2:4). When the marital "love level" declines, coldness sets in. You don't care about each other's problems. You don't listen to each other. You don't communicate.

Monitor your "love level" closely, for love is the very foundation of marriage. When love wanes, the foundation crumbles and you have nothing on which to build. If this has already been your experience, I rejoice to tell you that love can be rekindled! Let me tell you how.

Think back to the beginning. What first attracted you to each other? What qualities made you want to spend your lives together? What qualities or traits can you find to admire in your husband?

Communication must be restored. This involves listening as well as talking. It also requires a sincere effort to understand. Listen with your heart, picking up things left unsaid. Share your feelings. Be sensitive to his moods. Enter into his life. Probe a bit. Why is he that way? How can you help? Be open and honest with one another in every area. If you hide little things here and there, they will build up until once again you aren't communicating at all.

Respect is very important. Mutual respect is simply

showing honor, esteem, and consideration for each other. If respect has been lost, go to God in prayer and trust Him to help you. Win your mate's respect through your life. Because of the change in you, he might change also.

Forgiveness will cushion the rough spots. Be quick to forgive. Be quick to say "I'm sorry. I love you." There is magic in those words! If they are genuine, a husband is bound to respond. "Let not the sun go down upon your wrath. . . . And be ye kind one to another, tenderhearted, forgiving one another, even as God for Christ's sake hath forgiven you" (Eph. 4:26,32).

You must do whatever is necessary to make your marriage work and to make your marriage good. One woman was considering a divorce over problems caused by her job. Her husband wanted her to curtail her traveling in order to be at home with him at night.

"What am I to do?" she asked me. "Sell toothbrushes in a dime store?"

"You should do anything you have to do to keep your family together," I replied. "When your husband realizes that you genuinely love him, he will be willing to adjust, too."

There is another side to divorce, however. Perhaps you are the innocent one. In a night of rage he left, never to return again. Perhaps he was a bully. God never expects us to subject ourselves and our families to men who are cruel and emotionally unstable. Read 1 Corinthians 7 and be instructed in your own heart.

We sometimes tend to add to the heartache of divorced people by avoiding, neglecting, or even ostracizing them. Jesus did not react this way when He spoke to the woman at the well (John 4:7–42). She had five husbands in her past and was living unlawfully with a sixth man. But Jesus went out of His way to reach her with His divine love and the message of salvation.

Thank the Lord that the sins of her past were blotted out because of her belief in Jesus. Through meekness, understanding, and compassion, we need to befriend those who need us.

Love your husband. Love him when it's easy. Love him when it's not. Love him unconditionally. It will put iron in his spine!

14

No Way
Around Submission

According to Ephesians 5, a wife is to submit herself to her husband, even as the church is in submission to Christ. Similarly, a husband is to love his wife as Christ loved the church and gave Himself for it.

A woman will have no problem submitting to a Christian husband who loves her in this way. We women respond to love, affection, a wink, a pat, or just a loving look. If these are lacking in your husband, you will need special grace from the Lord to be submissive. Some men are not only lacking in love and kindness, but they are downright rude. (If they talked to waitresses in restaurants the way they talk to their wives at home, they would probably lose their front teeth!) Respecting this kind of man, and especially submitting to him, is no easy task.

Men can be changed, but not by wives. Please don't even try. My aim in this chapter is to share how I feel it is possible, in a variety of environments, to fulfill the commandment of Scripture to be submissive to your husband.

Submission to an unsaved husband is especially important. The promise of 1 Peter 3:1,2 is that through your chaste life and respect, you can win him to the Lord. Your life should be a consistent good witness; he is reading you like a book. Nagging him is the worst thing you can do. If he doesn't agree with your plans, don't pout and say, "You've ruined my whole day. I hope you know that."

If your husband does not want you to go to church, be prayerful and wait. You might try this approach: "Honey, you know I have been doing what you want me to do. Would you let me go to the Sunday morning service and take the children?" A husband would rarely be so cruel as to continually deny your requests if, in every other aspect of life, you are sweet, submissive, and loving. By submitting you are doing God's will. Through your submission and tenderness you can win him to the Lord. The Bible promises that! It is part of your reward.

To the Christian wife who has a Christian husband, your act of submission may or may not be easier. I am sad to say that simply because he is a Christian does not mean he will be a romantic, sweet, thoughtful person. Submission and prayer are without a doubt your solution, but let me give you some other helpful guidelines to consider.

First, count the aspects of your family life that are in disarray.

Have you stopped "dating"? This, of course, means taking time to communicate in a deep, personal manner. With the wild, mad rush of schedules, telephones, deadlines, and television, lack of communication is a serious problem for many people.

My husband and I always save some time each day to care about each other's thoughts, whether they be problems or blessings. Let me suggest that you take at least one evening each week to open your hearts to each other and talk frankly. Even if it means getting a babysitter so you can visit the "Golden Arches" or the Kentucky Fried Chicken restaurant, do it! It will be a wise investment. If your budget prohibits a weekly outing, consider having a cup of coffee or hot chocolate after the children are asleep and all work is put aside. As you talk, find out what you and he can do to bring back the romance you once shared.

Perhaps you have had money problems. Learning how to manage a strict budget will eliminate a major cause of disputes in your home. Even here, submission is important. My husband is a much better manager than I, so he has always kept the books. But if he had asked me to keep them, I would have taken a course in management and bookkeeping in order to do the best job possible. Try hard to follow guidelines that will please him and be equitable to the entire household.

Consider also God's commands about mutual submission in the area of lovemaking (1 Cor. 7:1–5). These verses sweep away any doubts about withholding your body from your husband or he his body from you. "Marriage is honorable in all, and the bed undefiled" (Heb. 13:4).

From childhood, Christian girls have been trained by their parents to save their bodies for "Mr. Right." For years they have said no to sexual advances. Thus, after marriage it may sometimes seem difficult to associate purity, righteousness, and holiness with the act of sex in marriage. But be assured that it is right and good in the sight of the Lord; sexual oneness in marriage is blessed and approved from heaven. In fact, God has given us a special caution not to withhold our bodies from our mates but to regard this act with special esteem.

There are many aspects of submission we could discuss, but every home is unique. As you seek the Lord's leading through prayer and meditation, He will help you discover and solve the problems that hinder your willingness to fulfill this command.

God did not make the husband head of the home because He loves the man more than the woman. This is simply the order He designed to ensure that the home operates smoothly. The wife and her responsibilities are just as important. A general is at the head of the army, but the organization will break down if subordinate officers and enlisted men are slack in performing their duties.

The Lord has given me a job to do and has set the boundaries within which I am to perform. He will reward me accordingly. When I stand before Him, He will not treat Jack more graciously than me. Although He has placed my husband over me, He loves us equally. Other religions have little place of honor for women, but Christianity uplifts us because the Lord loves men and women equally.

A husband is to honor and care for his wife as the weaker vessel (see 1 Pet. 3:7). Yes, he should highly regard her as befits a lady, never taking advantage of his masculine role. Serving as the head of the home makes him responsible for its spiritual climate as well as for his family's well-being. This automatically places upon him the burden of decision-making. Jack always seeks and respects my opinion, for which I thank the Lord. He also appreciates my sensitivity and input in various settings outside our home. We must be careful not to jump ahead of our husbands with our opinions. We must learn to think *before* acting or reacting.

My husband and I do not always agree, but we try to disagree agreeably! Our misunderstandings never last longer than ten minutes. (In the beginning days of our marriage, this was not so.) After giving my opinion, I entrust the matter to the Lord, praying that He will lead Jack to make the right decision. I know that the ultimate responsibility for the decision, right or wrong, falls on him. Although that is a great burden for him, it is a great relief to me. I am really liberated!

Women will never achieve true liberation through the feminist movement in this country. I believe in equal rights for women, but that is not the goal feminists are fighting for. Their hunger and needs are obvious, but their proposed solutions are wrong. They are missing out on the real rights of women—the rights we gain by submission!

Take time every day to read the Word and pray, asking the Lord for His love and grace to enable you to submit with joy.

Time to Pray

I got up quite early one morning
And rushed right into the day;
I had so much to accomplish
I took no time out to pray.

The problems just tumbled about me,
And heavier came every task;
"Why doesn't God help me?" I wondered,
He said, "Why, you didn't ask!"

I saw naught of joy or of beauty—
The day sped on, gray and bleak;
I asked, "Why won't the Lord show me?"
He said, "But you didn't seek!"

The Tender Touch

I tried to come into God's presence;
I used all my keys at the lock,
God gently, lovingly chided,
"My child, why didn't you knock?"

I woke up quite early this morning
And paused 'ere entering the day;
There was so much to accomplish
I HAD TO TAKE TIME TO PRAY!

—Author unknown

15

Becoming a "Helper Suitable"

A girl wrote to me, asking, "How can I marry a Jack Van Impe?"

My reply was, "I didn't marry a Jack Van Impe. I married a young evangelist who loved God with all his heart. I wanted to be a "helper suitable" for him.

The Lord blessed me with a temperament that could adjust to the circumstances of life. I felt very, very strongly at the beginning of my marriage that I wanted to adjust to my husband, to his life, to his ministry, and to do whatever was necessary to make our marriage good.

Jack and I are opposites in temperament, yet we enjoy many of the same things. The Lord put us together, and we blend beautifully. Adjusting my life to his did not seem hard, because to me Jack is a sweet example of everything a Christian man and a Christian husband should be. He is the head of our home, but he treats me like a lady. He is as thoughtful as when we were courting—surprising me with gifts, opening the door for me, and remembering birthdays and anniversaries. I have learned to be careful about commenting on things I like when we are shopping, because they may be under the Christmas tree!

He cares for my problems. He takes them upon his

heart, even if they are very small. He is never too busy for insignificant things. He wouldn't say, "Honey, I don't have time." With a million things on his mind, he calls in the middle of the day to say "I love you." He says his happiest time is coming home to eat and share his evening with me.

I try to be sensitive to Jack's moods so that he doesn't have to tell me if he has had a bad day. He doesn't get "down in the dumps," but he is human. And if he cannot express his humanity at home, where else can he? I don't feel that he has to be perfect. We love each other enough to understand the pressures and trials of life.

Jack is very understanding. There has never been anything I had to try to hide from him. We have talked a lot and we have laughed a lot. If we had not been able to laugh, some of the things that have happened to us would have seemed unbearable.

I thank the Lord that I have been able to keep my eyes not only on the Lord, but also on Jack. He has always had my utmost admiration and respect. He has been a fantastic husband. He has loved me.

In my Bible—a gift from Jack—he wrote, "To my wonderful wife who has made my ministry complete and fruitful, Genesis 2:18. Your loving husband." That verse from Genesis reads, "And the LORD God said, It is not good that the man should be alone; I will make him a help meet [suitable] for him." That is my number one priority—to be a helper fit for my husband.

Jack and I are one. I actually know what he is thinking. When something is bothering him, I respond. On the platform, Jack looks at me a certain way and I adjust the microphone. By experience I have learned much about public address systems and have been able to take this burden off my husband. If I see a possible problem arising, I try to intervene.

On one occasion a woman was looking for my husband after a crusade. She didn't know what to do about a motorcycle gang who had come forward at the invitation.

'I'll go with you," I said.

In the prayer room there sat a half-dozen, tough-looking youths, laughing it up.

"What's your problem?" I asked. "Why did you come?"

"Just to see what was going on," they said.

Jack had preached on hell. They said they didn't believe in hell.

Calm and controlled by God's Spirit, I leaned forward. "Well, you may not believe in hell, but one day you are going to be there." They were stunned. One by one I led them to the Lord. I may be small and appear fragile, but my Lord gives me strength!

My husband depends on me in many other ways. I remind him about things—both personal things and matters related to our ministry. (He has a personal secretary, but I am his personal, personal secretary!) He appreciates my opinion when he is shopping for clothes. This I consider a pleasure, not a chore.

Encouraging Jack is probably one of my top priorities. How do you react when your husband comes home discouraged? Perhaps he has lost his job. Do you explode? Or do you console him, saying, "Come on, honey, God has something better for us." Are you his greatest encouragement or his greatest discouragement?

The Lord has allowed you to become your husband's wife for a purpose. He plans every life so that we may use our gifts. Everyone has one or more spiritual gifts (1 Cor. 12:7,11) as well as natural gifts and talents, and God will give you ample opportunity to use these to help your husband. Work together; you are a team.

You can help your husband by being a good homemaker. Providing a clean, orderly home for us is one of my priorities, even though I am busy outside the home. Your home reflects your personality. If it does not exemplify cleanness and neatness, it suggests slothfulness. Even if your efforts go unnoticed, perform your duties out of love for your family. *Never expect praise, but always deserve it!* The atmosphere of the home is a reflection of your personality. I have walked into homes and sensed tremendous joy and love. Everything proclaimed that the woman really cared. She was a minister to her husband and to her children. Remember, your home is the greatest ministry you can have because you are molding lives.

You can help your husband by being a good mother to his children. Don't sell yourself short; a mother is very, very important. There is no influence in a child's life greater than yours. Behind Samuel was Hannah. Behind Moses was an obscure little mother who had more to do with the illustrious career of her famous son than any other person. Behind John the Baptist was Elizabeth. Behind Timothy was his mother, Eunice, and his grandmother, Lois. Your children need you to stand behind them, to give them instruction, direction, and above all, to point them to the Lord Jesus Christ.

You can help your husband by being a good listener.

Share his life and his burdens. Don't be so busy preparing dinner or caring for the children that you can't take time over a cup of hot chocolate to listen to him. Broaden your life so that you have things to share with him. Don't let yours become a television life that produces a boring person who has nothing to offer.

Your life need not be humdrum. If you cannot go out into the world, bring the world to yourself. Reading is a beautiful way to do this. Let me recommend a few of the Christian writers I enjoy: Helen Hosier, Eugenia Price, and Amy Carmichael. Books by Spurgeon, Ironside, DeHaan, LaHaye, Rice, and Tozer have meant much to me, as well as my husband's books. Quicken your mind and your spirit. Start your day with the Word of God and you will find strength and joy in the Lord to carry you through.

You can help your husband by giving financial help if necessary. If you cannot work outside the home, consider something you could do at home. Don't make him feel guilty by "sacrificing" to do it; consider it a pleasure to help. Many a woman makes the husband feel like a second-rate Christian because he isn't able to support his family.

The woman of Proverbs 31 was a working wife. She sold things for her husband's welfare. I have known many working wives. They were home when the children were small, but when the children were older, Mother went to work. Still, they kept the house immaculate and attended church regularly. They never neglected the family, and their husbands did not resent their wanting to help financially. The number one responsibility of a mother is to be a mother, but the church should not heap guilt upon the woman who has to work.

I know many women who have unselfishly adjusted their lives in order to be helpers suitable for their husbands. Let me mention just two.

Nancy Shelton, wife of evangelist Bob Shelton (my brother), was willing to go anywhere in the world with him—to the mission field in Viet Nam for many years, back to Michigan where he served as a pastor for another thirteen years, then on to Greenville, South Carolina, where they now maintain the headquarters of their evangelistic and radio ministries. Their children, Becky, Shari, and Dan, were all born on the mission field. But because of their mother's love and her sweet spirit, they never felt like persecuted "preacher's kids." They felt privileged to be the children of a minister.

Both girls married strong Christian men, and Dan is in a Christian college preparing to serve the Lord. Nancy stayed home until the children were grown. Now she travels with Bob and holds children's meetings. She adjusted her life for the sake of her family.

Let me add my personal thanks to Nancy, also. She generously shared her beautiful children with us, and they helped to satisfy my "mother instinct" as they stayed overnight and shared their secrets with me.

Marie Schuler, wife of evangelist Phil Schuler, was not resentful because her husband was away from home so much of the time. She was full of such love and joy that her daughters, Julie and Debbie, grew up without bitterness. They also married men in the ministry. Today Marie travels with her husband, playing the piano and organ superbly.

How far are you willing to go to help your husband? Remember, his calling is your calling, too!

16

Parenting: A Dilemma

Parenting can be a terrible dilemma. Some fathers and mothers are awed by the challenge of rearing children. They are almost fearful to proceed on their own, afraid to bring up the children with their own convictions and morals and faith. They are intimidated by what the so-called "experts" say in their books about childrearing.

You need not be afraid when you stand on the Word of God. If you do not know the Bible, begin now storing it in your heart. Let it be your guideline for life, and you'll give your children something to stand on, something to put their faith in.

Where should you begin? The Book of Proverbs is filled with instruction about childrearing. Training children through loving discipline is stressed throughout this entire portion of God's Word.

"He that spareth his rod hateth his son: but he that loveth him chasteneth him betimes" (Prov. 13:24).

"Foolishness is bound in the heart of a child; but the rod of correction shall drive it far from him" (Prov. 22:15).

"The rod and reproof give wisdom: but a child left to himself bringeth his mother to shame" (Prov. 29:15).

"Correct thy son, and he shall give thee rest; yea, he shall give delight unto thy soul" (Prov. 29:17).

Scripture makes it clear that we are to deal with our children the way the Lord deals with us. Hebrews 12 says the purpose of the Lord's chastening is to bring us to Himself, so that we might live holy lives. "Despise not thou the chastening of the Lord . . . for whom the Lord loveth he chasteneth" (Heb. 12:5,6).

Please remember this about the Lord's discipline: It is never done in anger; it is always in love. It is for our own good, helping our character to be conformed to His. This is the pattern for chastening children, also. Never discipline in anger, but always in love. Children should not be struck on the face or in a place where injury might occur. The bottom is well padded for a smack or two. Sometimes verbal discipline is sufficient, depending on the child. However, most of us have needed a spanking from time to time.

Don't leave your children to themselves. They *need* your guidance! From the time they are born teach them love for God, love for the church, love for our country, and love for the home. Teach them that home is a place where they can always come, a place where they will be loved and understood and treated with respect. Let them know you will always stand by them, no matter what the circumstances, but that you expect honesty and integrity from them.

Bringing your children up in the nurture and admonition of the Lord, as Ephesians 6:4 instructs, will demand that you get *involved* in their lives.

Time, a valuable commodity, must be given to your children. Mothers and fathers often make little ones feel they are in the way. If you have to miss a luncheon date because your child is sick, don't make him feel you are being sacrificial; rather, let him know you will cherish this special time with him. Begin spending time with your children when they are just babies. Show them they are wanted! As often as possible, include them in your social activities. Get involved in their schools and give them moral support. Don't let "Johnny" feel like a failure when he has lost a baseball game. My mother always assured me there would be a tomorrow, another time to try. She would *not* let me be discouraged.

Could it be that what's happening to our teen-agers today stems in part from their home environment? I have heard over and over again, "Oh, my mother and father don't really care what I do."

Look what's happening to our teen-agers. Drug addiction! Alcoholism! Premarital pregnancies! Satan worship! Suicide!

"What do you do when you see your son turn into an animal?" a California mother asked me. "He is a drug addict. He steals from me. He lies to me."

The U. S. Department of Health estimates that more than one million young people in America between the ages of twelve and seventeen have a serious drinking problem, and some 450,000 between ten and seventeen are classified as alcoholics.

One of four fifteen-year-old girls has had intercourse, and ten percent of all thirteen-year-olds have had sex, according to a report from the National Alliance Concern for School-Age Parents.

Some young people are entering into satanic relations. This is but another reminder that 1 Timothy 4:1 is coming to pass.

In some ways we are living in a horrible day. No wonder youths in staggering numbers are seeking escape through suicide!

Many young people live in a constant state of depression. When discouragement comes, they do not know where to turn. If you are not there to help and show them that the Lord has something better for them, they very well might resort to suicide.

Granted, most homes do not have the Lord as their stronghold in the day of trouble, but tragedies like these are occurring in Christian homes, too. I believe much of it is rebellion against hypocrisy in the home. Children demand and deserve honesty!

On one of our recent weekly telecasts I had the joy of interviewing Al Palmquist, a preacher-cop. He was ordained to the ministry but became a policeman with the prime objective of helping runaway youth. One of my questions was, "Why do so many young people run away from home?"

His answer startled me. One of the prime reasons young people leave home today, he said, is because fathers (and mothers) say one thing and do another. They do not carry through with promises. Perhaps Daddy promised to take them on a vacation. Junior told everyone in the neighborhood. Then Daddy became too busy, and Junior's boast of a grand and glorious vacation became nothing but a joke. This may sound like a very small thing, but when it is repeated in many aspects of life time and time again, young people become disillusioned and lose respect for their parents.

Being involved in your children's lives also means being informed about what they do and where they go.

Are you informed about the music they enjoy? Ephesians 5:19 is the guideline for Christians to follow. I also highly recommend David Noble's book, *Rhythm, Riots and Revolution*, as informative reading on this subject for every parent.

Are you informed about whom your children are dating? They should not date anyone who is not a Christian. Explain to them that they are not immune to falling in love with an unsaved person. In 2 Corinthians 6:14–18 we see God's plan for choosing a life partner.

Are you informed about what they are watching on television? The influence of television on young lives is of great concern to me. Actor and comedian Steve Allen, has said, "TV has gotten too dirty. Much of television is what I call junk food for the mind. I don't see any hope of lifting the quality of commercial television."

Yale University psychiatrist Dr. Robert Abramonvitz said, "Kids learn aggression from television. Anyone who has been brainwashed 15,000 hours via the television by the age of eighteen has learned aggression, profanity, and filthiness."

In one of his recent books, *Your Startling Future*, my husband quoted a report from the National Alliance Concern For School-Age Parents concerning sex among teen-agers. He believes the culprit is pornography in magazines and movies, and promiscuity on television. We become what we see, Jack states. How ridiculous, in light of the facts, to mourn over the moral problems of our children while we let them spend hour after hour in front of "the god with the glass face."

I praise the Lord for my husband's vision for helping

America through television. We are going into homes with something better than junk—the message of the Lord Jesus Christ.

To the Christian mother I would give these verses. "Ye that love the Lord, hate evil" (Ps. 97:10). "Have no fellowship with the unfruitful works of darkness, but rather reprove them. For it is a shame even to speak of those things which are done of them in secret" (Eph. 5:11,12). "Whatsoever things are true, whatsoever things are honest, whatsoever things are just, whatsoever things are pure, whatsoever things are lovely, whatsoever things are of good report . . . think on these things" (Phil. 4:8). "I will set no wicked thing before mine eyes" (Ps. 101:3).

In our day we need convictions that will help us to stand, no matter what. David Hume, an agnostic, was reproached by some of his friends because of his apparent inconsistency in going to church to hear the Orthodox Scottish minister, John Brown. Defending himself, he said, "Well, I don't believe all that he says. But he does. And once a week I like to hear a man who believes what he says."

We need to show the world that we have convictions. Your children need the security of your convictions. Sometimes when you say no, they can lean on that as an excuse for not doing something they didn't really want to do anyway—"My mother told me no." You have big shoulders. They can use you as a crutch, and there is nothing wrong with that.

Don't be afraid to say, "Mother is right," and show them what the Word of God says. Don't be afraid to say, "Mother was wrong. I'm sorry," when you fail. I used to think my mother and father were perfect, but at times they said to me, "I am sorry. I was wrong in telling you that you could not do that," or "I was wrong in telling you that you could do that. Please forgive me." Don't try to convince your children you are perfect.

Are you wondering how I know so much about *your* children? They have come to me by the hundreds and poured out their hurts. Could the following have been your son?

He sat in the front row, arms folded, a determined expression on his face, and a faraway look in his eyes. His shoulder-length blond hair and his attire set him apart from the neat-looking couple beside him—his parents, I imagined. Looking into the crowd I had just prayed, "Please, Lord, help me to sing and pray for people, not just a mass of nameless faces." Now God drew my attention to this young man, and he became my prayer target for that night.

As the service progressed, I sensed the power of God. How Dr. Jack preached! I noticed the young man's arms unfold and drop to his sides. His expression changed. The Spirit of God was getting through to him.

Before I knew it, the invitation time had arrived, and there was the object of my intercession standing in front of the platform waiting to go to the prayer room. His father moved quickly to his side and then his mother joined them. It may have been the first time in months they had really communicated. In a moment, they were all weeping, smiling, and embracing one another. Old barriers had been broken down by the love of Christ.

The following night my "answer to prayer" returned, accompanied by his girlfriend and four other friends, as well as his parents. The first one to come forward was the wide-eyed beauty he held by the hand.

Praise the Lord! He saw down deep into a young man's heart and met his needs. The young people of America and the world are spiritually hungry. We must give them the Bread of Life.

"What is the most important thing I can give to my children?" This question has been asked from one end of our land to the other. Parents, let me assure you it is not money, or luxuries, or anything tangible. *It is love.* Give them love, *the right kind of love.*

Real love is the essence of God's divine nature being exemplified in our lives. Without love we have nothing. We may have all kinds of understanding, knowledge, and faith. We may even give all our goods to feed the poor and become martyrs, but without love it profits us nothing (see 1 Cor. 13).

Let's see how love behaves.

Love "suffereth long." It is patient. It endures without complaining. Some ladies enjoy enduring so they can share it with their friends. How do you endure trials and affliction? Do you show patience at home? My, how it is needed!

Love "is kind." It is sympathetic, gentle, and polite. It cares.

One night a beautiful college girl from the University of Pittsburgh approached the platform and asked me if I would sign her Bible. "I will be happy to," I replied. Looking up momentarily, I saw in her large lovely eyes the most depressed look I had seen in a long time. I felt led to ask her directly if she knew the Lord as her Savior. Somehow I knew she would answer no. What a joy and privilege it was to take her to the back of the stage and lead her to Christ. Those sad eyes became calm, bright, and happy. The Lord always makes the difference.

The next night she came to me before the service and handed me a note, saying: "Please read this when you have a minute."

After starting the tape of the pre-service music, I excitedly opened the envelope. It read: "Dear Mrs. Van Impe: Thank you for caring."

I wanted to cry and sing at the same time. I bowed my head and thanked the Lord again for saving her, and prayed that my heart would always care. There are multitudes of people all around us, waiting for us to care.

Your family needs you to care. Above all, don't forget them.

Caring might also involve taking food to a neighbor who is sick, sending a card to someone in the hospital, or telephoning a relative who is lonely. Think of someone today for whom you can care.

Love "envieth not." It is not jealous. Can you truly rejoice in the praise of another without being jealous? I have yet to know a great man who envies another. The moment he envies, he loses his greatness.

Love "vaunteth not itself." It is not pushy. Do you try to lead the Lord, or do you follow Him? A lady came to me and said, "I have a beautiful voice, and I can't understand why God doesn't use me." God doesn't use those who push ahead of Him; He uses those who walk humbly with Him.

Love "is not puffed up." It is not conceited. Can you remain humble when you are praised? Are you mentally oriented to God's ways and God's grace?

Love "does not behave itself unseemly." Do you pout and explode easily when something doesn't go your way? Or do you display good manners, even to your husband and children? (Some families are nice to each other in public, but at home it is quite another story. I hope this is not true at your house!)

Love "seeketh not her own." It does not try to advance itself. Do you have a "me-first" attitude? If you have ever been on a New York City subway or on a city bus during rush hour, you know that the philosophy of many Americans is "me first." This should not be true of Christians.

Love "is not easily provoked." It is not hurt or angered easily. Does your tongue react first when you are angry? Be careful. You cannot take back what has been said. "The tongue of the just is as choice silver" (Prov. 10:20). What happens when you shine silver? You see your reflection. Your tongue can reflect the Lord in your life.

Once Jack and I stayed in a home where the mother criticized—from morning until night—the pastor and every other evangelist who had ever been in her home. I thought, "I wonder what she will say about Dr. Jack and me when we leave!"

At the end of the week, she asked me, "Rexella, please pray for my unsaved children."

I couldn't help thinking, "Oh, dear Mother, I wonder if you drove them away from the church by your tongue!"

Read this poem written by Eleanor Livingston Koot.*

Be careful my tongue, you are so little but strong;
So often your words are somehow all wrong.

---

*Used by permission.

You don't want to hurt, and yet there is a sting,
And so I must guard you, a worrisome thing.
How often I have wished that I could recall
Some harsh word spoken, and not meant after all;
And though I am forgiven, and have peace of mind,
I know there are sores such things leave behind.
So God, guard my tongue, and each word I say
So they may be pleasing to Thee, Lord, I pray.

Love "thinketh no evil." It does not imagine the worst of a word or deed. If your husband doesn't say, "Hi, honey," in just the right way when he comes home, do you pout for the rest of the night? Or if somebody says, "I like your dress," and you don't like the tone of her voice, do you think to yourself, "No, she hates it. I can tell by the way she said it."

Love "rejoiceth not in iniquity." It does not feel happy when someone fails. How do you feel about a friend who has fallen? Do you feel sick at heart and pray for her? Or do you pass it on, veiling the gossip by saying, "I am just telling you this so that you might pray more intelligently."

Love "rejoiceth in the truth." It is happy about the best in another person. Do you speak well about your friends? Sometimes we learn the worst about a person from her best friend. With friends like that, who needs enemies?

Love "beareth all things." It helps others with their burdens. Do you really bear another's burden as the Bible commands?

Love "believeth all things, hopeth all things, en-dureth all things." Do you have faith and endurance to carry out God's will and plan? Do you refuse to allow discouragement to nibble at your heels or at your husband and children? Do you stand fast in the Lord and in the power of His might—in all circumstances? Love doesn't give for what it can get. Love doesn't wait until it is deserved. Love is constant. Real love is unconditional. You can only give what you have. Receive God's love, and then be God's love.

17

The Great American Disgrace

America is fast becoming a pagan nation. Immorality, impurity, and iniquity all indicate that Jesus is coming soon. One of the prophecies Christ gave is found in Matthew 24:37,38, concerning eating, drinking, marrying, and giving in marriage—just as the people were doing in the days of Noah before the flood.

America is Sodom and Gomorrah revisited. Look at the corruption!

Premarital Sex

What a disgrace! Much of so-called Christian America has abandoned God's sacred marriage vows. The Lord does not wink His eye at premarital sex. Without reservation, the Bible is totally against the popular trend of living together without marriage.

One young unmarried couple who were living together accepted the Lord while watching our telecast. He turned to her and said, "Isn't it wonderful? We are saved." "Yes," she said. "There is the door." He left that night. Soon afterward they were married.

Sex outside of marriage is not God's way. We must

make a commitment to each other before the Lord in marriage before the sex act can be blessed.

Homosexuality

What dishonor! Much of so-called Christian America is approving homosexuality as a "normal alternative lifestyle." It is difficult for a candidate to be elected to an office in San Francisco unless he is a homosexual or has homosexual sympathies. Some churches are even ordaining homosexual ministers.

No matter how widely accepted this practice becomes, homosexuality is still sin. Read Romans 1:26–32. God justifies the sinner, but not the sin. Unconfessed sin separates us from a righteous God. We need to weep with those who weep, and hold out help and hope—but we cannot condone what the Bible clearly labels sinful behavior (see 1 Cor. 6:9,10 and Lev. 18:22).

Purity is the mark of a born-again person. "Beloved, now are we the sons of God, and it doth not yet appear what we shall be: but we know that, when he shall appear, we shall be like him; for we shall see him as he is. And every man that hath this hope in him purifieth himself, even as he is pure" (1 John 3:2,3).

Not long ago I led a lesbian to the Lord. She had come to our crusade time and time again in a city where we had ministered. However, she did not come forward. One night she asked if she could talk with me privately. "I want salvation," she told me.

I responded, "Let me ask you this: Do you *really* want salvation? Do you *really* want the Lord?" I don't believe you can force the Lord on anybody. They must desire salvation.

This girl had apprehensions because she was a lesbian. I explained to her that there are no practicing Christian lesbians, and that through the power of the Lord she could overcome this sin. She accepted Christ that night. "But what am I going to do?" she worried. "I am a lesbian."

It was a joy for me to say, "No, you are not! The Bible says 'such *were* some of you: but ye are washed' (1 Cor. 6:11, emphasis added). 'Therefore if any man be in Christ, he is a new creature: old things are passed away; behold, all things are become new' (2 Cor. 5:17). You can have a 100 percent cure!"

We have talked by phone several times since she received Christ. She is growing in the Lord and being used by Him in a singing ministry. What a marvelous testimony! "I haven't had any problems," she says. "I have had victory!"

Bestiality and Incest

How base a sin! Much of so-called Christian America silently tolerates men abusing themselves and their daughters. One dear lady came to me on the platform, weeping. She had caught her husband (a man respected in the church) in a sexual act with an animal, and then learned he had also had an affair with her daughter. I went home and wept. My heart and spirit were upset for days and weeks.

The Bible declares that men who have such sins in their lives will not go to heaven. From morning until night, they can insist that they are born again, but the Bible is absolutely clear that a born-again experience produces a different life. Again, "If any man be in

Christ, he is a new creature." There is not a Christian person who will make a practice of bestiality or incest (see Lev. 18:6,23).

Child Pornography

How shocking! Much of so-called Christian America is allowing children and teen-agers to be sexually exploited.

In an article entitled, "It Is Time To End This National Disgrace," Ellen C. Brownfield writes: "Slowly Americans have come to learn of one of the nation's fastest growing industries—child pornography. Recent Congressional Hearings have shown that the absence of specific federal regulation is permitting the mushrooming of an unsavory commerce that exploits an estimated 500,000 or more children as young as two or three years of age. The problem, as the Congress has recently learned, is staggering."

The Los Angeles police estimate that adults sexually exploited over thirty thousand youngsters under seventeen in 1979. Many of them were photographed in sexual acts.

In Houston, police found a warehouse full of pornography, including fifteen thousand colored slides of boys in homosexual acts.

In congressional testimony, the Odyssey Institute of New York noted that the Crossroads Store in New York City's Time Square carried *Lollitots*, a magazine showing girls fourteen through eighteen and children three through twelve—both nude and involved.

Babies! Just babies! You know, God has a special love for children. Jesus said, "Suffer little children, and forbid them not, to come unto me: for of such is the kingdom of heaven" (Matt. 19:14). He also said, "Whoso shall offend one of these little ones which believe in me, it were better for him that a millstone were hanged about his neck, and that he were drowned in the depth of the sea" (Matt. 18:6).

Child Abuse

Another disgrace! Often child abusers have themselves been abused as children. May I tell you about a girl I shall call Betty? She was eight years old when her mother married her stepfather. Shortly after their marriage, Betty awakened one night to see him standing nude beside her bed. Imagine this shocking introduction to the opposite sex at such a fragile age.

Betty immediately told her mother. The stepfather said he only wanted Betty to know what a man looked like. Somehow the mother accepted this explanation. But her stepfather continued to taunt her. When she was in the shower, he often would pull the curtains open. He never followed through with an assault, but Betty lived in constant fear.

Because she loved her mother and didn't want to ruin her happiness, Betty never mentioned another incident. Her mother never expressed love to her or tried to understand any of the problems she was going through. Betty struggled all alone.

The darling little girl became a bitter teen-ager. Knowing no love whatsoever at home, and being literally thrown out into the street, Betty married at seventeen. She was still a virgin, for which she later thanked the Lord. Often, improper advances from a father will result in a daughter's becoming promiscuous. Improper advances from a stepfather can plant hatred for men in the heart of a stepdaughter. So it was with Betty.

Her husband was a good man—not a Christian at that time, but a good man—who loved her. But Betty was filled with bitterness because of her past. Heaped on top of the fear and bitterness was guilt, although the former incidents were not her fault. She had had feelings of guilt ever since she was eight, when the incidents with her stepfather began.

When the Lord gave Betty a child, she spewed out her frustration by beating her until she was black and blue. Betty's husband never questioned the beatings; he seemed to feel that the child must have needed them. (Mothers and fathers should investigate such drastic discipline. It may be the parent, not the child, who needs help! *Discipline—biblical discipline—is not abuse!* God never intended for parents to strike children in anger or frustration. Discipline should always be administered in love, assuring the child that it is for his good and for the development of his character.)

Betty was searching. She knew her anger was wrong, but she didn't know how to express love or how to get rid of her bitterness. Soon after a second child came into the home, Betty and her husband were saved. Salvation, however, was not the complete answer for her. It was the eternal answer, of course. Her sins were forgiven and she had eternal life and the Holy Spirit dwelling in her heart. When the love of God came in, she realized how much she had been missing. She truly loved her children and wanted to be the kind of mother she had never had. But she had to deal with the bitterness. She sought counseling from her pastor, and God gave him wisdom in dealing with her problems.

Ultimately, Betty was able to overcome her fear through the love of God, for "perfect love casteth out fear" (1 John 4:18). God removed the guilt and dealt with the bitterness, enabling Betty to go to her mother and ask forgiveness, even though Betty had not been responsible for the constant state of chaos in their home. She also asked her stepfather's forgiveness. He broke down and wept. Betty felt as though a burden had been lifted; there is something cleansing and purifying about asking for forgiveness.

Today, the tenderness of the Holy Spirit is evident in Betty's life. She and her husband have a happy home and are serving the Lord. God gave them a third child, and they have shown him love, patience, and tenderness from the moment of his birth. Betty's life has been different since she found what God wanted her to have all along—the power to overcome bitterness and an unforgiving spirit! Today Betty sees her husband, her children, her friends, and even herself, in a new light—the light of God's love.

Your experiences may be different from Betty's in many respects, but the principles still stand. Bitterness must be dealt with or it will cripple you in your Christian walk. You must deal with your inner self, or you will find yourself lashing out at precious children, innocent wives or husbands, and friends—all to the destruction of your own well-being.

Confess your sin now. Ask God to dig it up by the roots. Otherwise, salvation—the eternal answer to your problems—will not wield much power in your daily experience. Ask the Lord for love enough to overcome all hindrances to a victorious walk with Him. He will begin today if you ask!

18

How to Have a Miracle

Prayer is the way to have a miracle. It is the key to real power. Prayer leaps over boundaries, balks at no obstacle, and reaches men everywhere.

Prayer is one of five channels through which the Holy Spirit works. The first is *what I am among men;* second, *what I do before men;* third, *what I say to men;* fourth, *what I give of my possessions;* and last, *what I dare to claim in Jesus' name*—through prayer.

One great preacher, Dr. M. R. DeHaan, has said, "I would far rather have the power of prayer to move the very powers of heaven than have the power of preaching to move masses on earth."

Dad Van Impe, Jack's father, heads the prayer ministry for our evangelistic organization. He spends five hours a day in prayer, taking before the Lord needs of people all over the country.

Why do Christians tend to neglect this greatest of all resources? Perhaps because we really don't know how to pray. The disciples asked Jesus how to pray and His answer gives us a beautiful model—The Lord's Prayer (Matt. 6:9–13). The prayer can be divided into three sections: the *uplook,* "Our Father," communion with God; the *inlook,* "give us this day," petition of

God; the *outlook*, "forgive us our debts," intercession with God.

Let me share some truths I've learned about prayer, beginning with the "uplook."

To pray "Our Father," we must be rightly related to the Lord. Until our souls have established communion with the Father, there can be no answer to our petition and intercession. This communion is established by being born again. Many people who pray "Our Father" are not God's children. This was once true in my life. *Be sure* that you are a child of God by receiving Jesus Christ.

Communion with God entails three essential attitudes: worship, submission, and confession. We worship when we pray, "Hallowed be thy name." We are saying, "Oh, God, how great you are." He is infinite; He is loving; He is omnipotent. Express your love to the Lord. Come to Him when you don't want anything and say, "I love you." It is important to sit and worship at the Lord's feet as Mary did. Martha wanted to serve Him, but Jesus rebuked her—not for serving, but for neglecting to precede her service with worship. We will serve more effectively if we take time to worship and commune with Him. He wants our love and our adoration first!

Submission is saying, "Thy will be done." Sometimes we come to the Lord asking not for His will but for His approval of our plans. We don't really want His will.

One girl asked me, "I am engaged to an unsaved boy. Would you pray with me about whether I should marry him?"

I said, "No, I won't pray with you about that. The

answer is already in the Bible. We don't have to ask the Lord. It is not His will that a Christian marry an unsaved person (see 2 Cor. 6:14). We don't have to pound on heaven's door to find the answer. But I will pray with you—if you will give him up—that this young man may be saved."

After much prayer and many tears, she returned the ring. A few weeks later, the young man accepted the Lord. I wonder if he would have been saved so quickly if she had been disobedient.

Sometimes we ask and receive not because we ask from wrong motives—for our own advantage (see James 4:3). The Lord has to say, "No, my child, what you are asking is not good for you." Three times the apostle Paul asked the Lord to remove the thorn in his flesh, but it was not God's will (2 Cor. 12:7–10). We must pray, "Thy will be done."

Confession removes all hindrances between us and the Lord. "If I regard iniquity in my heart, the Lord will not hear me" (Ps. 66:18). What are some hindrances that keep us from receiving answers to our prayers? Bitterness, jealousy, resentment, an unforgiving spirit, and many others. We are wasting our time praying if we are unwilling to get rid of what is between us and the Lord. "Create in me a clean heart, O God; and renew a right spirit within me" (Ps. 51:11) should be our prayer. How are we cleansed? "If we confess our sins, he is faithful and just to forgive us our sins, and to cleanse us from all unrighteousness" (1 John 1:9). Commit that verse to memory; it's a powerful promise.

Now, let's consider the "inlook." "Give us this day our daily bread." It pleases God when we petition

Him to supply our needs. Matthew 7:11 expresses what the Lord wants to do for us: "If ye then, being evil, know how to give good gifts unto your children, how much more shall your Father which is in heaven give good things to them that ask him?" God wants to bless us. However, He expects us to cooperate with Him and to be willing to work for the answer. If we seek to be good musicians, we must practice. If we ask for a good crop, we must prepare the soil and plant the seed. If we desire to see souls won to Christ, we must reach out to others and share the Good News. If we want food, we must work.

When we do all we can and our provision seems to fail, God goes beyond circumstance and performs miracles. In many of our outdoor meetings I have seen rain and tornadoes miss us because of prayer. In Pontiac, Michigan, the rain was all around us, but Wisner Stadium (where our meeting was in progress) was dry. Upon leaving the service, one man said, "I have seen the parting of the waters. It was a real downpour within three or four blocks of us." Through prayer, I have seen the hand of God protect us when we were threatened. I have experienced God's healing hand upon me personally time after time.

Many years ago I suffered repeated strep throat infections. Fearing that another infection would cause a rheumatic heart condition, the doctor wanted to burn the tissue in my throat. This might have meant the end of my singing ministry. At home, Jack and I got down on our knees and prayed. Once more I said, "Lord, if it is Your will, please heal me. If it isn't Your will, that is all right, too." I received a great peace from the Lord that He was going to heal me. I took the medicine the doctor had given me, and never had the surgery. And I have not had strep throat since. God gets all the glory and praise.

The greatest miracle in our ministry is seeing thousands coming to the Lord. The same God who answered the prayers of Elijah, Moses, David, Paul, and other great men of days gone by is the same God to whom we pray. When we meet the qualifications of prayer, putting our faith and trust in Him, God will answer.

Finally, the "outlook" or intercession involves praying for others. "Forgive us our debts as we forgive our debtors" demonstrates unselfishness. Do we really care enough about others to pray for them as we pray for ourselves? Are we willing to enter into their times of testing and trial with brokenness and tears? Can they entrust burdens to us with confidence, knowing that we will carry their needs to the Lord? Do we really pray beyond our own concerns?

The story is told of a young girl who said, "Lord, I am not going to pray for myself today. I am going to pray for others." But at the end of her prayer she added, "And give my mother a handsome son-in-law!" We just can't seem to end a prayer without asking for something for ourselves!

Much weeping may be required before we see the answers to our prayers. I will never forget a story about a woman who was praying for her two sons. "I can't seem to get an answer," she said to her pastor. "What should I do?"

He probed, "Do you know for sure you are born again?"

"Oh, yes," she responded. "I remember the day I opened my heart to Christ."

He then mentioned the points this chapter has touched concerning prayer. "Is there anything in your life that you know is standing between you and the Lord?"

"No," she answered.

"Is all known sin confessed?"

"Yes."

Then he said, "Have you wept lately?"

That question left her deeply disturbed. Even the salvation of her sons had not brought the tears nor the burden she should have had. That night in her bedroom, with tears streaming down her face, she fell on her knees and began to pray as she had never prayed before, "Save my sons!"

The boys came in after a night of carousing—wine, women, and song was their philosophy. Hearing their mother crying, they looked into her bedroom and saw her on her knees. It was too much for them. They decided, "If Mother loves us that much, we must accept Christ." The next day they went to the pastor and opened their hearts to the Lord.

I am deeply moved by stories such as this. Many women come to me in our meetings requesting prayer for unsaved husbands and wayward children. But one of my most vivid memories is of a weeping child. "Please, Mrs. Van Impe, pray for my mother and daddy that they will be saved." I was pleased to walk with her into the presence of the Lord. The throne of grace is ever open to our requests and prayers.

Prayer is as infinite as God Himself. We can dare to claim anything in the name of Jesus—not because of our goodness, but because of Christ. We can force our way through anything with the leverage of prayer, because God knows no limitations.

The thing I pray for most in my life is the fruit of the Spirit (Gal. 5:22,23). We need to pray for power—power to live consistent Christian lives and to win others to the Lord. We need to pray for understanding of the Scriptures. It's exciting to know that as we read, the Author is there to teach us.

Satan trembles to see the weakest Christian on his knees. Why? Because there is power in prayer!

God wants us to ask and believe. He specializes in rewarding faith. Can you commit your heartaches to Him? Your sick child? Your unsaved husband? God does hear us when we pray.

"I waited patiently for the LORD; and he inclined unto me, and heard my cry" (Ps. 40:1).

19

Guard Against
the Gremlins

The Christian life is a battlefield. Our adversary the devil "as a roaring lion, walketh about, seeking whom he may devour" (1 Pet. 5:8). He will create warfare in your soul. But don't despair, "for the battle is not yours, but God's" (2 Chron. 20:15). Your spiritual life will be marked by valleys and plateaus as you grow in the Lord and grow in grace.

Just where you are in your walk with the Lord, I have no way of knowing. And what gremlins Satan sends your way to rob you of joy and peace, I can only guess. Among women, I find these are his favorites: pride, depression, fear, an unforgiving spirit, and guilt. Let's talk about the first three in this chapter.

When I speak of pride, I am not talking about that innate ambition-related pride that makes you want to be and do your best for the Lord. I'm talking about the destructive variety that saw Lucifer thrown from heaven. God hates a haughty spirit. "Everyone that is proud in heart is an abomination to the Lord (Prov. 16:5). "Pride goeth before destruction, and a haughty spirit before a fall" (Prov. 16:18).

You don't have to be in a position such as mine, performing on the platform, to have the wrong kind of pride. Do you love the people in your church? Do you love some more than others because they are rich or nice-looking? This is something I had to deal with in the beginning of our ministry. (Read James 2:1–10 for biblical insight into this problem.)

Of course, this is not to say we won't have favorite people. Certain temperaments blend readily, and we are drawn to people with similar backgrounds and interests. But also we need to love those we aren't naturally attracted to.

Mrs. Booth, whose husband founded the Salvation Army, demonstrated God's love and meekness when she visited a prison. One woman—acclaimed as the meanest one there—would have nothing to do with her. Mrs. Booth tried to lead her to the Lord but could not break through her hatred. Before leaving, she leaned over and kissed her on the cheek. The woman couldn't sleep that night. The love of God began to penetrate that granite heart. Mrs. Booth was called back to the jail during the night to lead her to the Lord. Developing love and meekness is the way to conquer pride.

Depression is one of Satan's finest weapons. It is characteristic of my melancholy musician's temperament—the thing I have to fight most. I could have a serious problem with depression, hiding behind the excuse, "This is the way I was born." But early in my life I learned that if I were to be an effective servant of the Lord, I had to let the Holy Spirit control me, lest I be very low or very high emotionally. I cannot go into a crusade service in a low mood. Honest before the Lord, I would pray, "I have had a low day. How am I going to come out of this?" I found that when I asked, He would bring such joy to my soul that I wondered how I could have passed through such a valley. I went to the Word, particularly the Psalms, and discovered that no matter where I read, I received help.

Sometimes people feel "down" emotionally because they are "down" physically. However, most of us go through highs and lows. We are built that way. King David experienced extremes in his moods. We must allow the Holy Spirit and God's Word to carry us through those times.

Sometimes I come home very drained from meetings, traveling, recording, and taping for television. I have given my heart and soul; something has gone out of me and must be replaced. I must get alone with the Lord and give the Holy Spirit an opportunity to refill me. It doesn't take long for the Spirit to do His work!

I give God the glory for victory over depression. I have learned that all of heaven's resources are at my disposal, and my biggest weaknesses may be God's greatest opportunity to show what He can do. As John Newton put it, "Thou art coming to a King. Large petitions with thee bring."

Along with reading the Word, an effective cure for depression is praise. The principles of praise, thanksgiving, and rejoicing are taught throughout the Bible. "Be careful for nothing; but in every thing by prayer and supplication with thanksgiving let your requests be made known unto God" (Phil. 4:6). "Rejoice evermore. Pray without ceasing. In everything give thanks: for this is the will of God in Christ Jesus concerning you" (1 Thess. 5:16–18).

Even if you don't feel like thanking and praising Him, begin in faith. It will do more for you than for Him.

One time I became ill during a crusade and had to

stay at my parents' home. Jack was expected at our own home around 4 A.M. Monday morning, and even though our time apart had been brief it seemed like an eternity. About the time he was to arrive, I awoke and began to pray. Then I got out of bed, went to the telephone, and dialed our number.

Jack answered cheerfully.

"Sweetheart," I said, "I just wanted to call and say I love you and miss you." Just telling him the feeling of my heart did something special for me.

Likewise how sweet, how blessed, how peculiarly precious it is to come into communication with the Savior, saying, "Lord, I love You and praise You for all You mean to me." When you're feeling low, praise Him for His love, His mercy, His goodness, His kindness, His provision, His patience. Thank Him for who He is and for what He has made of your life through His grace. Watch praise chase away the blues!

Fear can be a devastating experience. It is one of Satan's pets. In 2 Timothy 1:7 we learn, "For God hath not given us the spirit of fear; but of power, and of love, and of a sound mind." If you are paralyzed by fear, you can be certain it is the work of Satan.

In God's precious Word there are more than 365 verses containing the words "fear not"—enough for every day of the year!

As we boarded a plane for Brazil, I noticed an attitude of concern in my husband. He is a man of steadfast faith, so I knew he was not afraid. I didn't question him, knowing he would share his burden with me when the time was right.

During the long flight I fell asleep. Suddenly I was awakened by his voice calling my name and him putting my seat belt around me. We were in a treacherous storm—no ordinary one like we had experienced many times before. The huge plane was being tossed around the heavens like a toy. The lightning was as brilliant as sunshine, even in the blackness of night.

For hours the plane bounced, heaved, and lunged over the Brazilian jungle. Strange as it may seem, I found myself at perfect peace during that horrendous night of uncertainty. I knew that the hands of my heavenly Father were beneath us, and my faith was placed in the power of His might. I was comforted as Jack prayed. Still, I wondered why he had felt such uneasiness about this flight.

Although my husband does not believe that fortunetellers and soothsayers have powers, he does believe demonic powers are real. Just prior to our trip, he had read a prediction in the Detroit *News* by a seer who had been 90 percent accurate in the previous year. This prognosticator (energized by satanic power, we believe), predicted that the greatest air tragedy in history would occur that Monday night in the area where we were flying.

Satan is powerful, but not all-powerful. Only our God is omnipotent. We believe a miracle happened that night—postponement of the predicted tragedy for the protection and safety of His saints and, above all, for His glory. The shocking ending to this story is that a plane did go down in that location on a Monday night, two weeks later.

"Ye are of God, little children, and have overcome them: because greater is he that is in you, than he that is in the world" (1 John 4:4). James says, "Resist the devil, and he will flee from you" (James 4:7). How do we resist the devil? Peter gives the answer: "Resist steadfast in the faith" (1 Pet. 5:9).

Take your fears to the Lord. You will find that the arms of the everlasting Father are never weak in sustaining His children. "Fear thou not; For I am with thee: be not dismayed; for I am thy God: I will strengthen thee; yea, I will help thee; yea, I will uphold thee with the right hand of my righteousness" (Is. 41:10). Look to Him in faith and enjoy sweet peace when the storms of life are raging. God our Father never sleeps!

20

The Healing Power
of Forgiveness

My husband had just preached on love when a woman came to me and shared her heartbreak. A man in her church had sexually assaulted her little girl.

"After tonight's message, I will stop hating him," she said. "But how do I forgive him?"

Forgiveness begins when we seek the Lord's face daily through prayer and the Word, allowing His love to fill our hearts until there is no room for hate. *Humanly* speaking, it can't be done. It must be a divine force, so almighty and consuming that it actually eradicates the hate Satan has promoted in the heart. We are human and we walk in the flesh. But don't ever forget the message of 1 John 4:4—He who is in us is greater than he who is in the world. And He who is in us is greater than we ourselves. We can't forgive, but God—in us—can!

Humanity killed God's Son. Still, He loves us enough to save us, and not only to save us but also to justify us—just as if we had never sinned. This is the kind of love He can give us to forgive others—just as if they had never hurt us.

In *It Feels Good To Forgive* (Harvest House, 1980), Helen Hosier states that the person who refuses to forgive "stands to be hurt and harmed the most."

Unforgiveness, she observes, "is emotionally, physically, spiritually and mentally destructive. It is keeping you from experiencing God's love and forgiveness."

An unforgiving spirit is the ground in which bitterness takes root. One night, following Jack's message on a salvation theme, a lovely young woman came forward for counseling. However, she just couldn't seem to say "I will receive Christ as my Savior." At last, the reason for her hesitation was stated: "I hate my father, and I won't forgive him."

How could she accept the love of our heavenly Father when she hated her earthly father? As she prayed and read the Word, the Holy Spirit did His beautiful divine work of melting her heart! Finally she said, "I do forgive him. I *want* to forgive him—oh, I love my parents. Please forgive me, Lord, please be my Savior."

How magnificent it was to see God's power change a person's heart before our very eyes! The Lord can work this miracle in your life, too, if you will allow Him to cleanse you through His Word and the communion of His Spirit. Ask Him to fill your life. Then there will be no room for bitterness and hatred! Begin a new life of forgiving right now. God can actually take away the hurt and blot out the very memory of it.

After we have been forgiven of so much, how can we continue to harbor grudges? The apostle Peter was concerned with forgiving, to the point of asking Jesus, "How oft shall my brother sin against me, and I forgive him? till seven times?"

And Jesus answered him:

I say not unto thee, Until seven times: but, Until seventy

times seven. Therefore is the kingdom of heaven likened unto a certain king, which would take account of his servants. And when he had begun to reckon, one was brought unto him, which owed him ten thousand talents. But forasmuch as he had not to pay, his lord commanded him to be sold, and his wife, and children, and all that he had, and payment to be made. The servant therefore fell down, and worshiped him, saying, Lord, have patience with me, and I will pay thee all. Then the lord of that servant was moved with compassion, and loosed him, and forgave him the debt. But the same servant went out, and found one of his fellow servants, which owed him a hundred pence: and he laid hands on him, and took him by the throat, saying, Pay me that thou owest. And his fellow servant fell down at his feet, and besought him, saying, Have patience with me, and I will pay thee all. And he would not: but went and cast him into prison, till he should pay the debt. So when his fellow servants saw what was done, they were very sorry, and came and told unto their lord all that was done. Then his lord, after that he had called him, said unto him, O thou wicked servant, I forgave thee all that debt, because thou desiredst me: Shouldest not thou also have had compassion on thy fellow servant, even as I had pity on thee? And his lord was wroth, and delivered him to the tormentors, till he should pay all that was due unto him. So likewise shall my heavenly Father do also unto you, if ye from your hearts forgive not every one his brother their trespasses (Matt. 18:21–35).

The Bible abounds with illustrations of forgiveness. It is the book of God's forgiveness, stemming from His boundless love for us (Rom. 5:8). Ephesians 4:32 states: "And be ye kind one to another, tenderhearted, forgiving one another, even as God for Christ's sake hath forgiven you." We are to forgive others because God has forgiven us; He commands us to do so.

Whom should we forgive? Everyone and anyone who has wronged us in any way—our brothers and sisters in Christ (1 John 3:14) *and* our enemies! Yes, even an unsaved person is deserving of our forgiveness. The Lord Jesus said, "Love your enemies, do good to them which hate you, Bless them that curse you, and pray for them which despitefully use you" (Luke 6:27,28). Later He continues, "Judge not, and ye shall not be judged: condemn not, and ye shall not be condemned: forgive, and ye shall be forgiven" (Luke 6:37).

In fact, if we do not follow God's command to forgive, He cannot forgive us and we will not receive answers to our prayers." And when ye stand praying, forgive, if ye have aught against any: that your Father also which is in heaven may forgive you your trespasses" (Mark 11:25). How important is the act of forgiving!

One of the most beautiful stories of forgiveness I have ever read is the Bible account of the prodigal son (Luke 15:11–32). This young man, one of two sons in a family, laid early claim to his inheritance and journeyed to a far country, where he wasted every cent on riotous living. When difficult times came upon that land, he was forced to feed swine just to stay alive! He finally came to his senses and decided to return home. He would confess his sin and ask to be employed as a hired servant on his father's farm.

As he approached the house his father saw him and, filled with compassion, ran to him, hugging and kissing him. The son's plan to become his father's servant was forgotten forever in the joyful festivities that followed. His father clothed him in the best robe available. The servants placed a ring on his finger and new shoes on his feet. The fatted calf was prepared by the family chef, and the household joined in a celebration similar to that which takes place in heaven whenever a sinner repents (Luke 15:7).

Unfortunately, the joy shared by the young man, his father, and the others fell short of including everyone. The Bible relates that the older son did not find the event an occasion to rejoice. In fact, he was angry (Luke 15:28). He would not so much as return to the house to welcome his brother home, even at his father's request. Instead, he cried "discrimination." After all, he had served his father for many years and had never been allowed such a gathering with his friends. This reaction bespeaks several facts concerning his character.

First, he was without concern. There is no account of his admonishing his younger brother as he prepared to leave home. He apparently did not attempt to dissuade him from making a wrong choice. Likewise, there is no indication that the older son ever spent any time searching for his brother or praying for him during his absence. His brother's whereabouts and welfare were probably the furthest thing from his mind, as evidenced by the fact that he had to ask the reason for all the excitement. Had he been praying for his brother's return, *expecting* God to answer, he would have immediately known the reason for the merriment. The father, on the other hand, saw his son returning "when he was yet a great way off" (Luke 15:20). He was watching and waiting with a heart full of forgiveness.

Second, the elder brother lacked compassion. Even when he learned what was happening he refused to extend his brother the simple courtesy of a "welcome home." Instead, he was bitter—possibly the result of years of sulking and self-pity because he had been forced to do the work of two on his father's estate. How sad that in a time of family crisis he looked inward rather than upward, thinking only of himself.

Finally, this brother was unwilling to forgive. The joy of being reunited with his loved one, the knowledge that the heavy hearts of his father and family had been relieved—all was lost because of an unforgiving spirit. Truly he was the loser. He was neither a true brother nor a true son of his father. Likewise, a Christian cannot be filled with joy until he is willing to call "brother" (or "sister") those whom God calls "son" (or "daughter").

If you would know the peace and joy of constant communion with the Lord; if you would understand the concern of God for all people; indeed, if you would have the power of God upon your life and service for Him, learn well the lesson taught in 1 John 4:7, 8: "Beloved, let us love one another: for love is of God; and every one that loveth is born of God, and knoweth God. He that loveth not knoweth not God; for God is love."

Then, and only then, can you experience the healing power of forgiveness.

21

How Do You Handle Guilt?

"How do I handle the guilt of having lived in adultery for twenty years?" a woman asked me.

First, I led her to the Lord. Then I assured her that the past was forgotten, just as if she had never sinned. The blood of Christ cleanses us from all sin (1 John 1:7). The moment we receive Him, we start a new life. Our past is never remembered again.

God has promised, "Their sins and their iniquities will I remember no more" (Heb. 8:12). It is often said that God casts our sins into the sea of His forgetfulness and puts up a sign: "No fishing allowed."

However, Satan can use guilt feelings to rob us of our joy and effectiveness for Christ. Often he brings to our remembrance the past with all its ugliness. To overcome this assault, we must have full assurance that we have been forgiven of our sin (the promise of 1 John 1:9). Then we must dwell with Christ in daily communion, constantly aware of His glory and the joy of knowing that He wants to use us in spite of our past.

Having received forgiveness in Christ, we must next forgive ourselves for our failures. This is what I believe the apostle Paul was thinking when he wrote, "forgetting those things which are behind, and reaching forth unto those things which are before" (Phil. 3:13).

I picture Paul sitting down one day and, in a state of despair, declaring, "I am the worst of sinners." Then the Holy Spirit whispers, "Forget those things which are behind. You did your best. You did all that you could do, and God knows all about it, so forget all the things which are behind you. Press toward the mark for the prize of the high calling of Christ" (see Phil. 3:13,14).

The Holy Spirit makes the same statement to us today. Do all that you can now and leave the rest with the Lord. Look toward the future.

Our thought processes can work to our advantage or to our disadvantage. I believe that "Gird up the loins of your mind" (1 Pet. 1:13) means don't allow yourself to look back, especially on failure and on the sins for which you have been forgiven. Think on those things that edify the soul. Philippians 4:8 expresses beautifully the kinds of thoughts that should fill the minds of Christians: things that are true, honest, just, pure, lovely, and of good report.

It is very hard for me to reflect on my life. I have found it much healthier to look ahead, reflecting only long enough to say "Thank you, Lord." I never wallow in guilt, even for two minutes. I will not allow my mind to do that.

I learned to control my thoughts at a very young age. After singing in church one night, I was angry with myself because I thought I had done a bad job. My brother Bob asked, "Did you do your best?"

"Yes, I did," I answered.

He simply said, "Well?"

"Thank you, Bob," I replied.

That lesson stuck with me. During the first year of

our ministry, I fought those angry feelings when I didn't do a good job. The Holy Spirit seemed to speak to me as Bob had done.

"Did you do your best?"

I did.

"Well?"

I realized that although I might not do a superb job every night, I could do my best . . . and that's all that is required.

Each of us struggles with personal failure. Remember Paul's frustration in Romans 7? The things he wanted to do, he didn't do. The things he didn't want to do, he ended up doing. That is also true in my life. I echo his cry, "O wretched man that I am! who shall deliver me from the body of this death? I thank God through Jesus Christ our Lord" (Rom. 7:24,25).

You may feel guilty over a son or daughter who has strayed away from God. Don't condemn yourself by asking, "Where did I go wrong?" Did you do your best in rearing him or her for Christ? Then claim the promise of Proverbs 22:6: "Train up a child in the way he should go: and when he is old, he will not depart from it." Don't spend the rest of your days in regret. Rather, seek God's guidance in helping your child now. Forget the past and let your love and concern show through your prayers to the God who cares. Hands off—God is at work!

We will never be perfect in this life, but it's good to know we have been forgiven—not only for our past sins, but also for our daily shortcomings and the weaknesses that will cause us to fall short of the glory of God throughout life on earth.

Think of it! We are forgiven . . . past, present, and

future! "There is therefore now no condemnation to them which are in Christ Jesus, who walk not after the flesh, but after the Spirit" (Rom. 8:1).

No condemnation! And no guilt!

22

Be True to Yourself

My life has been exciting, unique, meaningful, and blessed. Many times I have looked toward heaven and asked, "Lord, why did You choose an immigrant boy and a little hillbilly girl and put us together to blend our talents and our love for You?" I cannot explain why He has chosen us and blessed us, save to say that we have honored Him and His Word. Why did He choose David, the young shepherd boy, instead of his older brother? Servants are chosen by the providence of God. Only He knows why.

A lady I had never met once wrote to me seeking forgiveness. She had seen me on television and thought, "Oh, the glamor of it all." There is glamor on the platform, but please, don't ever aspire to fill someone's shoes unless you are willing to walk in them all the way. There is a price often to be paid for a blessing.

God has plans for you. Ask Him to reveal your strengths and unique qualities. As you recognize these areas, work to cultivate them. Your life may not catch the world's attention, but it will influence your immediate world and be a blessing to others.

An evangelist's wife said to me, "My husband wants me to be like you."

"Oh, no! Please, be yourself," I begged her.

It is wrong for any husband to want his wife to be like another. God made each of us with our own potential. Your beauty is in being who you are. In our first year of marriage I had to learn who I was and what my potential was. You must do the same.

Most of this book has been devoted to married women. Even as a young bride, I had a great burden for them because I saw much need in many of their lives. Wives have often confided to me, "You are the only one I can talk to." The Lord began to deal with me about sharing with other women some of the experiences of my years with Jack. I wanted to be close to them and help them on a personal basis.

Ladies' luncheons proved to be a wonderful idea. During our crusades, pastors' wives and their guests join me for lunch. This gives me an opportunity to become acquainted with them and to speak informally, perhaps touching a need in their lives. Many women have been saved and countless others have found renewed strength in the Lord. Afterward, husbands have come to me and said, "Thank you so much. Our home is really different."

My prayer is that through the thoughts shared in this chapter, God will meet a need in your life. Let me begin with those young ladies who are thinking about marriage.

You will save yourself much heartache by marrying a *Christian*—a young man who is willing to follow God's order, taking his place as head of the home and allowing Christ to be over him.

Also, make certain that the man you marry is a man of *character*, who chooses to do right, possesses wisdom, and allows the mind of God to work through him. (His reaction in a crisis is a real test of this attribute.)

Finally, marry a man whose *countenance* is special to you. This does not necessarily mean he is handsome in the world's eyes, but you will think he is because when you're with him your heart turns over!

These are my "three Cs" for choosing a husband. Then, most important in your marriage, make Christ the *center* of your home.

I would also like to speak to those women the Lord has chosen to remain single. You are very special. The Lord has planned your life this way for a specific purpose. Seek His face daily to learn why He has allowed you—yea, blessed you—with a special ministry. We married women devote much of our time and our attention to our husbands, but you can give all your time to the Lord (see 1 Cor. 7:32,33).

You may find the single life difficult to accept. It is natural to want someone to love you and hold you here on earth. Still, you must remember that the Lord is not trying to take away something that would be good for you. He knows you intimately, and He has a special reason for wanting you to remain single. Your ministry has been planned with great care in heaven!

Whether you marry or remain single, God has made you just as you are and has planned your entire life around His will. If you rebel, you will be rebelling against God. In whatever role He has placed you, be true to Him and to yourself. Allow Him to develop your personal ministry. You may be surprised what He can and will do through the comforting power of His Spirit if you will surrender yourself. Really now, aren't you just a little curious about His plans for you?

Let me also warn you: The job will be too big for you to handle alone. You must always remember that Christians are merely instruments through whom the Holy Spirit works.

Often I hear individuals say, "I would love to give the Lord my talents and serve Him, but what do I have to offer? My abilities are so insignificant and few."

In Albany, New York, a young boy quietly approached me prior to the crusade service. With eyes bright and shining, he said, "Here, Mrs. Van Impe, this is for you and your husband."

He handed me a warm loaf of homemade bread.

"Thank you!" I exclaimed. "And did your mother make this for us today?"

"No," he replied. "I did."

I wanted to hug and kiss him for his beautiful expression of love. Not wanting to embarrass him, however, I touched his arm and said, "Oh, thank you, son, so very much."

And you ask, "But what could my small talent and gift mean to the Lord when the needs are so great?"

A small boy gave his loaves and fishes to the Lord and five thousand were fed. God will abundantly bless and multiply your gifts when they are given in love.

His reserves are never exhausted!

23

Hurry Up!
I Want Him!

The little town of Nara, Japan, houses the world's largest image of Buddha. We were interested in seeing this representative of pagan worship and planned a trip to the temple during our stay in the country. Surprised to see thousands of worshipers filing in and out of the shrine, I experienced an almost uncontrollable desire to run ahead of the throng, spread my arms in front of the huge doors, and shout, "Please don't go in! It's just an image of wood and mortar. This god cannot hear you, or see you, or help you. I have a *living* Savior I want to tell you about!" (See Ps. 135).

Once inside, I felt warm tears on my cheeks as I watched the people pray before the image—stories high and imposingly impressive. I felt frustrated that we could not share the gospel message because of the language barrier. During the train ride back to our hotel I observed the beautiful, kind faces of the Japanese. I wanted to be more than just friends; I wanted to tell them of the dearest Friend of all—the One who loved them enough to die for them. Millions around the world have never heard. This is so even in America, a land filled with churches.

A church bus driver in St. Louis, Missouri, was transporting children to Sunday school. It was the

Christmas season, and he began telling his young riders the wonderful story of Jesus' birth in Bethlehem's manger. As he spoke, one little girl leaned toward him and asked in a puzzled voice, "Sir, what is a Jesus?"

Oh, how my heart broke when I heard this story! Did the precious little soul think that Jesus was a piece of furniture, or a lollipop, or a new toy she might find under the tree on Christmas morning? How sad that she had never been told that the babe born in Bethlehem was the God-man, the Messiah who came to save His people from their sins!

It is unthinkable that thousands, perhaps even millions, in America do not know the meaning of John 3:16: "For God so loved the world, that he gave his only begotten Son, that whosoever believeth in him should not perish, but have everlasting life."

One summer when I was home from college, I taught a children's Sunday school class. On our special "Decision Sunday," I gave the girls a strong salvation message. All of them—about a dozen in number—wanted to be saved! One at a time I led them to the Lord, asking each, "Do you really want Jesus in your heart?"

When I came to the sixth girl, she urged, "Hurry up! I want Him!"

Because of the preparatory work of the Holy Spirit, many can hardly wait to receive Jesus! Are you taking time to introduce Him? My heart's desire in prayer has always been that I would never lose the joy of seeing people respond to the invitation during our crusades, and that God will keep me ever concerned about reaching people on a one-to-one basis. The Bible does not say that the angels only rejoice when multitudes are saved, but over "one sinner that repenteth" (Luke 15:10).

I do not believe we must corner everyone we meet and ask, "Are you saved?" I believe that if we walk in the Spirit (Gal. 5:16), He will lay individuals upon our heart and open the doors of opportunity as we talk about the Lord. I have dealt with women for years. Some were ready to come to Christ immediately. Others were saved only after long periods of patience and prayer. Truly, we must continually rely on the leading and power of the Holy Spirit. After all, it is God who gives the increase (1 Cor. 3:6).

Just the other day a lady asked me, "Why are you different?" *Thank you, Lord—an opportunity to witness!*

I have also visited door-to-door. I believe in this approach. The Lord sent His disciples out two by two, under the anointing of the Holy Spirit. We must always pray, discern the Spirit's leading, and then respond accordingly.

Our responsibility is to be living witnesses. God's responsibility is to draw the unsaved to Himself (John 6:44). In our crusades, my husband and I work very hard. We pray very hard and we weep very hard. But when we go home at night, we sleep. Our responsibility as Christians is to work, pray, weep, and then rest—leaving the results to the Lord.

Judy was a beautiful salesgirl in her mid-twenties. She seemed to be seeking a purpose in life. Although she was a church member, she was not saved. As we talked one day, I saw a rerun of my own life in hers. I sensed that she wanted to talk about more than the cosmetics she sold. Immediately, I began praying for Judy and witnessing to her about Christ. I gave her our booklets and records. I also felt led to introduce her to my niece, Becky, one of our secretaries and a soulwinner.

A friendship developed. Becky carried a special burden for Judy, weeping for her soul. She invited Judy to lunch and presented God's plan of salvation. Judy was not ready. Becky then invited her to revival services at her church. At the last minute, Judy cancelled. Was she losing interest, or was the devil working overtime to keep her from Christ? Somehow I felt an urgency to reach her *now*!

I asked Judy to lunch and told her how I longed for her salvation. To my surprise, she looked up and said, "I want to be saved, Mrs. Van Impe, but I don't know how." I again explained the plan of salvation, but Judy did not want to pray in the restaurant. We went back to my car. I told her she could receive Christ before returning to work. With great sincerity and humbleness of heart, she asked Him to be her Savior. I thought I heard the bells of heaven ring! Another child in the kingdom!

God has provided a special place in my heart for little ones. I always scan the audience for their fresh, innocent, and sometimes mischievous faces. Children are impatient as they wait for the service to begin. They are curious about the accordion, the evangelist, and the lady. They talk to me.

"How old are you, Rexella?"

"Can I marry you?"

"I like to hear you sing."

"I like your daddy" (meaning Jack, of course!).

They are so tender and sweet. I can fully understand why Jesus wanted little children to come to Him. How thrilled my heart is when they do. Deep within I whisper, "I've been praying for you, little one." At that moment my joy is double: A soul has been saved and a whole life spared the devastation of sin.

As we left our crusade in Beckley, West Virginia, the last voice I heard was that of a little girl calling to me as we walked away into the darkness. Her childish voice was like music, "Come back soon, Rexella!" Precious little one, I'd love to come back and tell you more about the sweetest name I know—Jesus, my greatest Friend, the sinless Son of God who changed the world and who changed my life!

All around us there are those who are just waiting for us to reach out to them with the gospel message. Many are waiting for the story of salvation through the Lord Jesus, saying, "Hurry up! I want Him!"

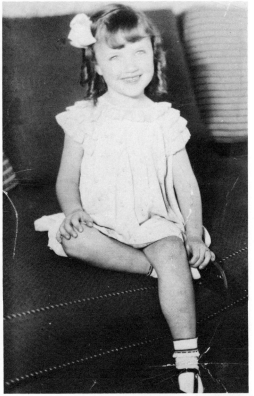

This is how I looked at age five, when I started my singing career. I sang for anyone who would listen!

Visiting brother Bob at college. (L to R: Don—10, Bob—18, myself—14, mother and father.)

Grandmother Shelton (center, age 77) with my parents. I remember how she loved to sing and play her harmonica during quiet evenings.

Grandmother Hodge (age 81 in 1968). She was always available for talk and comfort.

My mother and father at the time of their fiftieth wedding anniversary.

Jack's parents celebrating their fiftieth wedding anniversary.

Jack spends hours in study and prayer for each message. When he speaks, he is a man in action.

We enjoy a laugh during studio taping.

People have told us they appreciate the humor, too.

At the piano in a San Diego crusade (1977).

I love singing for the Lord.

On the weekly TV program I enjoy interviewing guests, such as Dr. Paul Freed of Trans World Radio.

The much-respected soloist Jerome Hines appeared with me at the TV taping in New York City's Carnegie Hall, summer 1980.

Our 1979 TV Christmas special was taped in Nashville.